To Keith,
Good luck,
D Beal 1984 Gold Medal

Spike!

by

Doug Beal
with Marc Katz

AVANT
BOOKS

ISBN Number 0-932238-30-0
Library of Congress Catalog Card Number 85-71269

Slawson Communications, Inc.
3719 Sixth Avenue
San Diego, CA 92103-4316

Oak Tree Publications
9601 Aero Drive
San Diego, CA 92123

Avant Books™ is a trademark of Slawson Communications, Inc.
Cover Design and Photo Layout by Ed Roxburgh, The Word Shop, San Diego
Interior Design by Mike Kelly, The Word Shop, San Diego
Editorial coordination by Linnea Dayton
Photographs courtesy of and with permission from Focus West, Volleyball Monthly, and Bruce McAllister
Cover photo provided by Focus West

Contents

To my dad: I may be getting there.

"Even the most courageous among us only rarely has the courage for that which he really knows."

"The formula of my happiness: a Yes, a No, a straight line, a *goal*."

from *Twilight of the Idols* by
Friedrich Nietzsche, 1888.

Chapter 1.

Dressed in gold.
Winning the Olympics.

Dusty Dvorak blocks the ball to the floor and we are Olympic Gold Medal champions.

"We won, Bill, we won!" I scream. But I can't hear my own words — the din in the Long Beach Arena is too much.

Bill Neville and Tony Crabb, my assistant coaches, embrace me. The team has played almost perfect volleyball against Brazil's team. Without distractions or controversies, they've earned the most one-sided victory ever in the men's Olympic volleyball gold medal match.

Athletes are superstitious and normally don't celebrate until a game is over. But as soon as the score of the final game reached 13-6 in our favor, we celebrated anyway. I think it was Neville who first rejected protocol.

"Congratulations, Doug, we did it!" he shouted. "We've won!"

"Oh, this is fantastic!" yelled Crabb. "Oh, I can't believe it!"

I had always prided myself on reacting properly to every situation. But this was different. In spite of the protocol and decorum that generally dominate the sport, I wanted to scream, yell, punch the air with my fist for everyone in the world to see who and what we were.

Yet those men in the blue blazers, the stoic International Volleyball Federatio officials, sat directly behind our bench. Those men — the legends of volleyball — formed the jury that made the decisions about a match that a referee couldn't make. They were also a reminder of how to behave.

And there was still some coaching to do.

Aldis Berzins was on the back line to serve for the gold, but we didn't win the point. Steve Timmons made a great blocking move and we should have had a stuff, but the ball went off his fingertips.

"Geeze, we ought to get Waldie in," I said to Neville. "Yeh, I'll go get him," Neville said.

Our team had a policy that subs would warm up during matches so they wouldn't go in cold. At the Olympics, the warmup area was nearly 30 yards away. We had to call the guys by telephone the way baseball managers call the bullpen. This time though, Neville ran to get Marc Waldie, and the sub was made.

Waldie went in, but before he could serve, the action had to stop while a wet spot on the floor was mopped. The wait was tense — *intense*, and the pressure on Waldie was enormous. Everyone in the arena was standing in antici- pation of the final point. Some coaches can replay a whole match even years later, point by point. I can't; but that point I remember, even though we didn't win it. The tension was like what you feel during the last pitch in the bottom of the ninth in the World Series of all World Series!

Timmons served, and the last point, the winning point, was elusive no more. Neville, Crabb and I were ecstatic. We knew we had won. I was babbling. When Dvorak blocked for the winning score, I was screaming. This was too much. The place was bedlam. None of the 12,000 fans could sit down.

That moment of victory is freeze-framed in my memory.

We won. Somehow, we all had known we would. As we walked onto the floor before the match we knew we were well prepared. We felt a certain calm, a confidence. Feelings don't ensure a victory, but we felt in control even before the first serve.

The match went just the way we wanted it to. And then it was over, and we were the Olympic gold medal winners!

We had been through so much as a team; so many controversies and so much hard work. We'd earned this wondrous moment of victory, and everything else faded away as we reveled in it.

At the end, our players gathered at the net to have their first picture taken as champions. I was at one end of the court talking to friends when I heard my name being called.

"Doug, come on, you've got to be in the picture."

They didn't have to do that, but the players insisted I join them. They hadn't always liked many of my coaching decisions, but they wanted me to be a part of the picture. We were a team; the victors' picture had to be complete.

That might have been the best moment of all.

Chapter 2.

Getting there was only half the fun.

Most people saw the Olympic victory as a single event. We played, we won. It wasn't quite that easy.

So much had happened over the previous eight years. When I accepted the head coaching assignment, the U.S. Volleyball Association was experimenting with a whole new approach to its national teams. Their policy had always been to assemble teams at the last minute and force-feed international competition, under the illusion that we could field a world-class team.

The United States did have what appeared to be strong teams in many sports during the 1950s, a period of naivete toward amateur athletics. Other countries had not yet developed their athletic prowess. None had a comprehensive training program. The United States won, in many cases, with numbers. Other successes came from sheer individual effort, not because officials provided the best of athletic opportunity. And so we had a Jesse Owens, Wilma Rudolph, Billy Mills, Glenn Davis, several great decathletes, and others.

Looking for an edge, Europeans began training their teams year-round, and the time and effort paid off. Eventually, the United States had to change its approach to amateur sports also. We tested the European style on the volleyball court, and it worked. But the road to the Long Beach Arena was not always smooth. Along the way, we struggled for sponsors and had trouble with officials, players, parents, the volleyball community, the media, and my own stubbornness.

My attitude and my philosophy of winning through consistent hard work and a highly structured and disciplined program alienated some of my players. Some left; some stayed and simply disliked me. I even quit once. Inevitably, a few irate parents tried to have me replaced. I saw our training concept, as well as

3

my job, threatened. And I was undiplomatic with the media, which didn't always place me, or volleyball, in the best light.

Winning the medal put those struggles behind us, though. Now we need to concentrate on the practices that allow our players to rise above imperfect situations. Even when our preparations go well, we still have to expect the unexpected. The outcome of athletic events is often based on factors beyond the control of the players or the coach — a referee or linesman makes a bad call, injuries occur, or the ball takes a funny bounce.

Some people don't like to talk about luck in relation to sports, but it's there. A perfect play in football fails because the receiver slips and falls running a pass pattern. A grounder hits a pebble on a baseball diamond and bolts off just out of reach. A dead spot on a basketball court causes a missed dribble. And who can predict injuries? I can't. I can only be prepared for them. To me, there is a luck factor.

What isn't luck though, is everything else. In the match with Brazil, we had all the things we could control in place. We were prepared and felt that if both teams played the best they were capable of playing, we'd win.

Our loss to Brazil in the round-robin portion of the Olympic tournament was overemphasized, but we weren't too concerned about it. Some people actually suggested that we orchestrated the defeat to lull everyone into believing we weren't such a good team. There are a lot of reasons we lost that match; but a planned defeat is nonsense.

"I don't know what's the matter with Karch," I said to Neville during the first Brazil match. "He certainly isn't the guy I've been watching the last four years."

Kiraly Karch wasn't playing up to par, but he wasn't the reason we lost. We made enough mistakes to feel safe calling it a team loss.

Kiraly's attitude, though, was magnificent. In the locker room after the loss, he put it all together for the other guys.

"Forget about this match," Karch said. "We didn't need to win to get into the medal round, so don't worry about it."

I said the same thing, but Karch's statement reinforced it. The guys really paid attention to him.

Obviously, we didn't play with the same intensity as Brazil, but we certainly didn't throw the match. Simply put, we were already in the medal round and Brazil had to beat us to get there. Yet after the tournament, the hottest topic of conversation was our first-round match with Brazil. Knowledgeable people in this country and around the world questioned that match.

Korea, knocked out of the medal round because of our loss to Brazil, was also miffed. When we went to Korea for a tournament after the Games, they accused us of losing just to keep them out of the medal round. They thought we hated Koreans!

Really, the people who say those things can't understand volleyball very well. It's almost impossible to conceal anything from international teams that see each other so often. After all, we had played Brazil many times.

But you don't throw matches. It's a waste of skill to create your own difficulties. Even using an odd lineup or trying different tactics can be risky. We did change our lineup, but that had more to do with motivating our players for those matches we absolutely had to win. Our first match against Brazil wasn't one of them.

We weren't ready to send Pat Powers back in at that point, and Paul Sunderland had played well. So we went with Sunderland instead. And Craig Buck was still having some foot problems, so we kept him out of the starting lineup, too.

We didn't spend a lot of time motivating the guys to win that first match with Brazil. It would have been nice to win. We wanted to win. We just didn't have to, as Brazil did, to get into the medal fight.

What were we going to say to ourselves? We had to win? We didn't. Carl Lewis didn't have to continue making long jumps after he jumped far enough to win. We didn't have to beat Brazil to reach our goal.

Lewis was criticized for his decision, and so were we, even though we didn't make a conscious choice to lose. We weren't saving ourselves for later, but we didn't want to peak too early emotionally, either.

We played hard. We wanted to win. Ironically, those people who were saying we threw the match were actually congratulating us for doing so. They thought it was a clever ploy to distract the Brazilians. Again, nonsense!

By the final match, we were ready, emotionally and physically. We were also in a position of advantage. A number of elements put us there.

Worldwide, the top three or four teams have been very close in ability and results. During the tournament, this worked in our favor. Korea was probably the third best team, an aspect Brazil may have overlooked. While looking ahead to their pool match with us, Brazil didn't spend much time preparing for Korea, and promptly lost. The Brazilians couldn't adjust to Korea's big outside hitter, Kang Man Soo, who had one of the greatest hitting matches in Olympic history that night.

Korea, then, did us a favor. Beating Brazil was important. After we beat Korea, 15-13, 15-9, 15-6, Brazil had to beat us in the last match of the round-robin, to stay in the race for a medal. We had already qualified for the medal round, and it was difficult for our players to focus and get motivated for Brazil. But on the other side of the net, Brazil was playing for its life.

It is difficult for Americans to understand the enormous pressure on Brazil's players during the Olympic Games. Their volleyball team was the single greatest hope for their country to win any gold medal.

In Brazil, volleyball is replacing soccer as the country's No. 1 sport. There, a *Placar* magazine poll shows that the most popular athlete for the past two years has been a volleyball player. And the most popular events have been volleyball events.

Brazil filled a 100,000-seat stadium for a volleyball match against the Soviet Union — in the rain. When our team played there after the Olympics, we sold out three matches that were broadcast live by four television stations and nine radio stations. People were scalping tickets outside the arena for huge prices!

The Brazilians had finished second at the previous World Championships to the Soviets, and with the Los Angeles boycott by the Soviets and Eastern Bloc countries, Brazil became the natural favorite. This was especially true in their own country.

So Brazil, on August 6, played a match they refused to lose. (It reminded me of Don Larsen's perfect game in the 1956 World Series.) In my mind, there was little chance they could repeat that performance. And because they won, it was also unlikely they would make any strategy changes for the final match. We had lost, and were prepared to try different things.

Another significant factor in our favor was *how* we lost that first match with Brazil. The match was much closer than most people realized, particularly the first two games. Those were the longest games in the entire tournament, lasting 96 rotations. A game of 36 rotations is extensive. Although we lost, 15-10, 15-11, 15-2, we forced Brazil to go to great lengths to beat us.

When the time came to play the gold medal match, we had the right players in the right positions, all were mentally prepared to win, and those tactics that worked for us in our march to the Olympics were in our match plan.

Our player changes centered around using Powers and Buck in the starting lineup, something we had not done in the pool match against Brazil. Powers had to sit out a couple of matches to calm down, even though he was one of our better players. He wanted to do too much, to be too perfect, and if he didn't perform the way he thought he should, he put too much pressure on himself. By leaving him out of the lineup, we showed him the team could play well without him. That tactic eliminated much of his stress. Then, when we really needed him, he went in and was outstanding.

Buck needed some pumping up, too. When motivated and concentrating, as he was in the semifinal against Canada, Buck is devastating. So we decided to let him play, give him our confidence, and ride on his shoulders in the final.

Using Powers and Buck turned out to be nice moves.

One other major factor that helped us was probably psychological. In the first match, Brazil served very impressively. Their jump-spike serve, in particular, caused us some problems. As a coaching staff, we decided to handle this serve with a simple change in our serve-receive patterns. We focused on this in practice and worked on blocking the serve to protect certain sections of the court. If nothing else, it gave the team something to hang on to; a new tactic, a mental boost.

We blocked only one serve in the gold medal match, and that was early on. But it gave our team a lift and effectively neutralized Brazil's tactic, at least in our players' minds. (Rule changes are made two years before an Olympics and go into effect just after the Olympics. In the next Olympics, in Korea, no blocking of serves will be allowed. Before then, we'll need to develop a spike-serve, too.)

Brazil wasn't the only team facing the final match under pressure. There was a significant amount of pressure on us as well. Many volleyball officials feel the sport will become more important worldwide and will benefit from the extensive media coverage and improved public relations that will result if American teams do well and Americans support them. Those officials had been waiting long and patiently for the United States to develop a championship team. I think we more than met their expectations in Long Beach during this XXIII Olympiad.

Another consideration was that we were playing in Los Angeles, the home town of most of our players. If our plan didn't work — if we didn't win — local support of our program might have been in jeopardy. Finishing second, or third, might not have been enough. Companies hiring athletes want to hire winners. We had made major progress in our jobs program and other aspects of our year-round training center, and winning the gold medal would only further enhance our efforts.

There were other reasons for us to win. Mainly, it would help the status of the sport in this country. With our high visibility at the Olympics, pressure might be put on high schools to start more volleyball programs.

Volleyball for men in the United States is below the level of an emerging sport. Fewer than 50 university programs are active in the country. There are fewer than 50 players of legitimate international ability here, and only a handful of coaches with international experience.

That isn't all that worked against us.

We had never, in the history of men's volleyball, won a medal in a world tournament — not in the World Championships, the World Cup, or the Olympics. No other team in the world has ever taken such a quantum leap! We won, in spite of the pressure. And considering the state of the sport in the United States, what we accomplished in so short a time is spectacular.

Some people thought qualifying was enough. Some thought reaching the medal round was enough. But to us, the coaches and players, only the gold medal was enough.

That isn't to say just reaching the Olympics wasn't a thrill. There is so much more to that event than just winning. The emotion and aura of playing in the Olympics is almost impossible to describe. Unless you're involved in an amateur sport in which your ultimate goal is four years away, it's hard to appreciate the pressure and focus involved in striving for this goal. Even professional athletes, who have so much riding on the Super Bowl, World Series, or other championships may not fully appreciate it because their opportunities arise every year. Their cycle repeats every season. "Wait 'til next year" is always the cry.

Next year? Next year the amateur athlete may be selling insurance. "Wait 'til four years from now" is not a rallying cry. Four years is a long time to wait if you blow it.

Today, the pursuit of excellence in the Olympics is a four-year ordeal that can end at any time. A better athlete may replace one who has trained for years. Injury or age may cut down others. Or, as in the last two Olympics, boycotts can shatter a dream.

To stay on top, to be ready when the time comes, amateur athletes rarely, if ever, have an off season. Our volleyball team trained, and trained hard, day after day, year after year, and only in the last year did we get a chance to compete for our goal. We put in nearly 2,000 hours a year in the gym, and our players trained from 3 to 12 years at that pace. We practiced, played, trained, and worked all at the same time. Our players worked at their jobs as well as pursuing excellence in athletics. They achieved the ultimate under the most demanding circumstances. They split the focus of their attention. Our players were able to successfully deal with the business distractions frequently cited as the downfall of professional athletes.

That's why, during the Olympics, I frequently told people I just wanted to figure out a way to put those 12 days in slow motion. So much time and preparation was funneled into so short a fulfillment.

I wanted to feel everything, to experience everything. I walked through the village where we stayed, and ate in all the cafeterias on the USC campus. I rode the buses. At the Long Beach Arena, I wanted to feel the energy of the building. I sat in an empty locker room. I walked out through the tunnel onto the floor. There I visualized the people in the stands and heard them cheering for my team, and me. I felt proud.

I didn't want it to end. It was something I've lived my life for since the early 1960s when I first got involved with volleyball. I still played other sports, basketball and baseball, and ran track, but volleyball was something special. It was magnetic to me. It was my passion.

When I became a good player, I thought I understood volleyball at a different level, almost as an art form. I knew as a coach I could pass along some of my knowledge to others.

It frustrated me when I was coaching at Ohio State to hear administrators talk about major sports and minor sports. It's certainly offensive to coaches, but even moreso to athletes.

No serious athlete considers his sport "minor" or likes to hear it diminished or ridiculed in that manner. He gravitates to a sport by his abilities and successes. A football player is no more dedicated than the decathlete, the rower, the fencer, or the volleyball player. They all take their sport seriously and try to be their best. Many strive to reach the elite level of their sport, not only in their own country, but in the world. Whether the media or the public perceives a sport as "big time" or minor shouldn't influence the athletes or the others closely involved in the sport.

This second-class citizenship isn't just a problem encountered in colleges. It seemed to me the women's volleyball officials tried to do much the same thing. When we *did* get attention before the Olympics, we were compared unfavorably to the women's team. I can remember reading numerous articles about our women's team that mentioned the men's team. According to the media, we weren't training as many hours, our players hadn't sacrificed enough, our people hadn't spent as much time in the program. We hadn't been together as long. We didn't practice as many months of the year. We didn't travel as much. I saw example after example of promoting the women's program at the expense of the men's. Frankly, I'd have been happier to wallow in obscurity.

It frustrated me tremendously. It was foolish. Of course our players had worked as hard as everyone else did to achieve excellence at our game. What bothers me, though, is the poor sportsmanship this attitude demonstrates.

Out of respect for all athletes, we made a conscious effort never to criticize the women's program publicly. We tried to teach our players to respect other athletes whether they liked them or not.

One of the toughest issues we had to deal with among our players was how to handle the aftermath of an outstanding play. In a volleyball environment, it's common for athletes to get involved in banter or even provocation under the net, sometimes to the point of demeaning players on the other side. Since there is no physical contact in volleyball, emotional outlets often are achieved by screaming, pointing, and intimidating stares. When players celebrate the failure on the other side of the net rather than the success on their own side, it creates negative competition.

I try to instill a more positive attitude. If you block someone, don't scream at the player who was blocked. Turn your back on that player and celebrate with your teammates. That's the nature of a team game. The best thing you can do is ignore an opponent. Our team certainly didn't like it when other players ridiculed us, but we didn't always see it from the other side.

I prefer to train athletes to play against themselves. If you only want to be better than an opponent or a teammate, you limit yourself. Each time you touch the ball, make it the most important touch of the game. That's the philosophy. Don't watch the other players to see how they're doing. Don't worry about the scoreboard. Be the best you can be on each play, every point, every contact; then forget it, it's over.

Celebrating with your own team creates internal enthusiasm — it's positive and it generates energy. Playing against yourself improves skill and sportsmanship. These were important concepts for us and something we worked hard to learn.

By the time we arrived at the Olympic Village, we were a mature team, able to handle most situations well.

Of course, there were many trying times. When you drive and push people hard, some feelings get hurt. I remember being embraced by virtually every player after we won, even though some still don't care for me. Some disagreements and conflicts die hard. But the euphoria of winning the gold medal superseded everything.

A lot of people said we couldn't do it. Many said we couldn't do it my way. Then, we did.

Our success over the two years before the Games was rewarding. I knew I could put together a winning team. I knew the United States could win on the international level, long before we won the gold.

The decisions my staff and I made were the right decisions. We ran the program in the best interests of the players, and all of volleyball, both on and off the court. I didn't need to win the gold medal to be vindicated, but it certainly didn't hurt.

What critics sometimes don't understand is that the unsuccessful things we did eventually paved the road for the 1984 success in Los Angeles. The foundation had been laid in 1977 and 1978 in Dayton. Winning the gold medal and doing it in Los Angeles, the hotbed of U.S. volleyball, was a special victory. And we did it in front of so many people who hadn't thought we could.

More than that, there were other people in those stands who were behind us all the way. I have pleasant memories about so many people in the U.S. Volleyball Association (USVBA), the linesmen, scorers, referees, and others who give their time and support.

Not everybody gets to live their fantasies. Most people only see an Olympic event on television or read about it in newspapers. I was lucky. I was in the arena, urging my team on, trying to remember how I should act, and going crazy.

It was one of the peak experiences of my life.

Even Neville wasn't prepared for the gold medal experience. He coached the 1976 Canadian team, but they had no chance of winning. The sensation is entirely different when you're coaching a winning team. And this team was capable of winning.

I was only sorry some of the attention was taken off the team's athletic skills and shifted to meaningless controversies. I don't think that was fair.

A lot has been said about my abrasive personality, as well as the conflicts between my players and me. Some folks in the media even found it significant that I maintained an emotional distance from my players.

I think it's interesting and amusing when so much is written by writers who don't know much about the people or the situation they write about.

Our whole program, and many of our problems, can be explained very simply. We developed a program to make our men's team the best in the world. To do that we had to adhere to a philosophy and a set of principles that were the foundation of our program. Any individual who couldn't conform was expendable, but the philosophy, and rules, were not. When players wanted to train under an alternate set of criteria, we frequently got rid of them. We stuck to our principles and succeeded.

Volleyball isn't the most popular sport in the United States. And our program isn't the most popular in the sport. But our nation's volleyball elite are dedicated athletes who train hard. They work all year for four or more years to play in these games. Not many other athletes have trained harder than the 12 players we lined up on the floor to play Brazil in the Olympic volleyball final.

Sacrifices were made by all, the coaches, USVBA staff, and the players. They all shared in the sacrifices, and they all shared in the victory.

Sure we were controversial. Sure we made decisions that didn't please everyone. But we felt we had to in order to win a championship never before won by a U.S. team.

There may be lots of ways to win, but they're only conjecture at this point. I'm not sure we did everything right, but I am sure we did almost everything right.

After all, we won.

Chapter 3.

You can't tell the players without a scorecard.

Generally speaking, players make the difference between winning and losing. Other factors, however, do contribute significantly — for instance, the staff and support groups that surround the players.

It's only natural for me to have strong and positive feelings about my staff and the job we did. But I also want to acknowledge the role the USVBA played in our victory. Long mired in the old way of assembling teams and then wondering what went wrong, the USVBA adjusted its policies to the new order, and we benefited. The association and its executive director, Al Monaco, stood behind us during good times and bad.

Monaco, hired in 1973, was the first paid executive of the USVBA, and his office then was in San Francisco, his home town. I didn't care for him at first. I thought he was overbearing, abrasive, and curt, and that he made many hasty decisions. I realized later how he was benefitting the association and began to change my opinion.

Now located in Colorado Springs, he and the USVBA have been extremely supportive of us. They stood by us during all the controversies and gave us credit for all the victories. From the start, they wanted our program to work, and when it did, the officials sanctioned further expansion that should translate into even more success for volleyball.

My assistant coaches, Bill Neville and Tony Crabb, were also invaluable to our program. Bill is my best friend, and there's something special about sharing a winning moment with someone that close.

We went through some hard times together during our years in San Diego, and Bill has suffered some difficult personal times as well. We talked and worked our way through it all and came out winners. Bill has so much integrity, he deserves that success. He has saved me from making bad decisions so many times. He is the conscience of our program. I have more respect for Bill Neville than for anybody else in volleyball.

Tony Crabb, who joined us later, is such a tremendous counterbalance to our staff. He makes terrific contributions and is responsible for many of the technical improvements in our team. The players don't always understand Tony's efforts. Yet, he is a professional, always trying to find ways to make our match plans better. Always challenging the traditional ways of playing. He makes us constantly reevaluate our thinking.

Our use of statistics, videotape analyses, and scouting for the Olympics — most of it done by Tony — allowed our team to play more effectively. We felt we were better prepared than our opponents, a step ahead. I think Tony, as much as anyone, is responsible for that.

Ultimately, however, a team wins because of its players.

It was my job to bring the players together and mold them into a team, a job made more difficult by the free-spirited individuals involved. These are intelligent, high-strung athletes with inquisitive minds, possibly the toughest kind to coach. They want to know why, and it's trying sometimes to disrupt play to explain the reasoning behind each move.

It also takes patience to integrate conflicting personalities. Our team wasn't another Oakland Athletics of Charlie Finley's time, but not all our players were buddy-buddy, either. And often, my way of doing things led to conflicts. Some were unfortunate; some were unavoidable. Many were petty.

"You never smile," my players told me.

"Smiling never won an athletic event," I countered.

"Let up, Beal. We've practiced enough."

"Just a few more reps, guys. You play the way you practice. I don't want to hear you'll play better in a game. Show me now."

"Beal, you never want to have fun."

I am not there to be a buddy. Let them make friends among themselves — that's important.

When choosing a team, a coach has to pay attention to physical and athletic abilities, but also to the ability of players to mesh. From the start I knew there would be problems choosing a team. Some of the men simply couldn't get along with each other. Even if they didn't come right out and say so, it was obvious when we had certain combinations on the court. Sometimes in basketball, when one player is not liked or respected as a player, the ball is never passed to him. To eliminate one player on the floor from an offense, especially in volleyball, is suicide.

Eventually, the players did work together because everyone's goal was the same. They realized a need for one set of rules and one command post.

It's true that I didn't like all my players. I can't believe any coach does. Some of them were petty or stubborn, some complained just to complain, about the practice schedule, travel — anything — and some used the most minor excuses as reasons for poor performance. But as long as players did what they were told and worked as a team, their idiosyncrasies were mere aggravations to be accepted. If a player had the ability to perform and conform, he stayed and played.

Neville, Crabb, and I tried to put aside our personal feelings. Being a buddy was no way to do this. I didn't want to make decisions based on friendships. It took quite a while to settle on a team, and the players' viewpoints were often different from ours. They had problems with us, we with them. Yet at the end, we had the 12 best team players this country had to offer. Differences aside, they are champions, and should always be remembered as such.

Dusty Dvorak, a strapping 6-foot-3 setter from Laguna Beach, California, played at USC and was one of the most talented and important players on our team. He was a four-year All-American and the NCAA's most valuable player in 1980.

As good as he is, he presented special, and at times seemingly insurmountable problems. Outwardly, he has tremendous composure and presence and is a supremely confident athlete. But Dusty is also thin-skinned, high-strung, and temperamental. He is difficult to work with from a coach's perspective because he only likes to play with certain people, and his opinions of players might change weekly.

For example, Dvorak complained about playing with a certain player and about his impact on the team. But when we cut that player, he wanted to know why and publicly questioned the decision.

Dusty is also sensitive to criticism, so we had to be careful how we talked with him. Yet, when instruction is presented carefully, he takes it well and can inject it into the team's play effectively.

We put up with him not only because he is such an outstanding talent, but because he has the sense to stop short of total disruption or direct confrontation with the staff. He was our first captain in San Diego; but after our Outward Bound experience, we decided to have yearly elections for captain.

Outward Bound, a wilderness experience designed to bring the team closer together, was held early in the winter of 1983. Dvorak was completely against the project, and when he asked to leave in the middle of it, we didn't argue. We told him he could do so, under two conditions: His position on the team might not be guaranteed upon his return, and he had to tell his reason for leaving in front of the entire team.

He didn't leave, which says a good deal about him. Dvorak isn't always in agreement with what we do or ask him to do, but he fits into the system. In spite of being difficult to coach, he is a special talent and a credit to the team.

He controlled himself admirably during the Olympic Games. He blocked effectively and played better defense than normal. He also integrated well into our offensive system. We wouldn't have won the gold medal without him. He's clearly one of the top three or four setters in the world. In fact, I think he's the most complete setter the United States has ever produced.

Dave Saunders, an All-American from UCLA, is one of three players on the team from Pacific Palisades, California. He is 6-3 and a model team member, a player I can't say enough good things about.

Early on, I didn't think Saunders would make the final cut. I even had to be talked into giving him a tryout. His physical abilities are minimal, but he has a tremendous arm swing, one of the best on the team.

Saunders is a good server and good passer, and he isn't afraid to swing hard and aggressively, even on match point. He's what we call a "terminal" hitter — the ball seldom remains in play after he spikes. He has an aggressive nature that makes him perfect as a role player, especially coming off the bench.

Saunders works hard and has never caused me a moment's loss of sleep. Although he didn't play much in the Olympic Games, people like him are valuable on any team. If coaches had 12 guys like Dave Saunders, they would enjoy walking into practice every day. He may be closer to his real potential than anyone on the team.

Another UCLA player from Pacific Palisades is Steve Salmons, a 6-4, 200-pounder. He began his athletic career as a basketball player, as did many of our athletes. Salmons was persuaded to switch to volleyball in high school. Later, in 1979, he was part of UCLA's historic first undefeated NCAA championship team.

Salmons replaced Tim Hovland when Tim left. Hovland may have been quicker and better offensively, but Salmons worked harder and contributed significantly more to the total team effort on and off the court.

He helped raise practice intensity and the quality of competition between the first and second teams. We actually wanted him before he was available. Because of a back injury he missed most of 1980 and 1981. He also wanted to complete his school work. We didn't get him until January, 1982.

Salmons hates to lose, and it doesn't matter if he's a first-stringer or a sub. He competes equally hard in both situations. He was known to create confusion on the court occasionally, either by forgetting assignments or from lack of finesse, and when he left his area or decided to play a ball that wasn't really his, other players got out of his way. Salmons could have been a linebacker or a pulling guard. He could hurt you, and he never stopped going for the ball.

Off the court, his life-style was a bit irresponsible.

We did manage to rechannel some of Salmons' behavior, though. In 1982, we told him we wanted him to become a spokesman at civic affairs. He is quite good at that, and it helped change his objectionable behavior.

I wish we could have given him more playing time, but I expect him to be a major contributor in the next quadrennial.

Paul Sunderland, another former basketball player, is 6-6, 190. One of our old-timers, Paul was 32 at the Olympic Games, and had been with the team longer than most of the players. He joined the National Team in 1975, even before the program moved to Dayton, and retired after the Games.

Sunderland is from Malibu, California. He played basketball for two years at Oregon, then transferred to Loyola Marymount in Los Angeles where he concentrated on volleyball.

He is a smooth athlete and a consistently good outside hitter with a lot of range. He was a starter for the team virtually from the beginning, although over the years, age and injuries took their toll. He has exceptional ball control and is very agile for his size.

Sunderland never gained a leadership role, but he could play numerous positions well and was an important stabilizing force on the team. Thoughtful, dedicated, and supportive, he genuinely loved being a member of the National Team. He did as he was told, and he worked hard.

He played his best volleyball at the Zone Championships in Indianapolis in 1983. In one sense, he may have reached his physical peak there. Later, he developed ankle problems and underwent knee surgery. He played in more international matches than anyone in the National Team's history. Even with his injuries, he always contributed to the team effort and added a degree of quality and maturity to our team.

I have to laugh when I think of Rich Duwelius. He spent almost as much time on the National Team as Sunderland, and also retired after the Games. Duwelius had an odd personality. Coincidentially, we gave him an odd number.

The other players on the team called him "delirious." After practice at an Olympic training site a few days before the Games began, he made a telephone call and couldn't get himself out of the phone booth. That's the kind of guy he is.

Duwelius, at 6-6, 195, was one of the few on the team who was not from California. A fellow Clevelander, he studied at Ohio State and was an easy guy to find a job for because of his engineering degree.

Many times I didn't think he would make the final team. He was especially confounding during competition when he experimented on court with new techniques. He's a good athlete, though, quick and strong.

Duwelius has horrible ball control skills — to this day I don't think he can handle an underhand pass — but he can receive difficult serves all night long. He isn't smooth, but he is a well-trained blocker who puts a lot of pressure on our other middle blockers to perform well. He played some great matches in which he absolutely dominated.

Duwelius didn't get to play much in the Olympics, but he played well leading up to them. We had four good middle blockers, and we just couldn't play them all.

On my first international coaching trip, to Canada in 1977, Duwelius played some great volleyball. They couldn't stop him. But I told Neville — who was coaching the Canadian team then — that Duwelius wouldn't be with us very long. Jim Coleman, our advisor at the time, also heard my remarks and reminded me of them at the '84 Games. "I see you still have Duwelius," he said.

Yes, we almost cut Duwelius, but I'm glad we didn't.

Steve Timmons is another player we nearly cut. In fact, we did ask him, from time to time, to play with other teams that represented the USA. He has had a real roller-coaster ride with us.

From Newport Beach, California, Timmons is 6-6, and a former USC All-American like Dvorak. He joined the National Team as an undergraduate in 1981, but didn't play often during the first three years.

I wasn't sure about his attitude, whether he was always giving us his best effort. And unfortunately, he didn't have good ball control skills. Yet absolutely without question, he developed our team from a good one into a great one during 1984. We put him into the lineup against Cuba during our 1984 tour there and he really got our team going.

Timmons was the only player on our team asked to attend the World University Games in 1983, and he wasn't very happy about that. He thought he was being cut and demoted. We thought it was a great opportunity for him to get a lot of playing time. I've got to give him credit, though. It was a tough thing to do, but he went and the experience he gained was helpful.

Usually, a coach can do something like that to a player once or twice. Timmons got it two more times. We kept him off the roster for our Pre-Olympic Tournament in August, 1983, and sent him to the Pan American Games, while the first team went to the Soviet Union for the prestigious Savvine Tournament that September. As late as October, he was not considered one of our top 12 players, let alone a starter.

"How many times can we do this to this guy?" Neville kept asking.

"I don't know," I said. "I guess we can do it until he's ready, or quits. Either way, we win. If he improves, we're better. If he doesn't, it's best to find out now we can't use him."

Neville coached that Pan American team, and from then on Timmons improved. Neville was close to Timmons, so it was a good decision to put the two together.

Originally, our backrow offense depended on Hovland. When he left, we didn't have the hitters there, until Timmons. We developed a very sound backcourt attack with him. His awesome back row hitting and tremendous quickness helped us win the gold.

We did have a problem with him during the Olympics. He was so excited and anxious, he started to hyperventilate and we had a tough time keeping him from passing out. He made it through, though. He's a good kid and has a bright future in volleyball.

The most imposing player on our roster is Craig Buck, a 6-8, 210-pounder from Tarzana, California. He played college volleyball at Pepperdine and is a most interesting character.

Buck began in the national program with our junior team, and back in those days, he was just a gangly kid who couldn't even do one pushup. He disliked working hard, but was easy to coach. He's a bright and basically good-hearted kid who wants to be liked. We decided early on he was going to be a key player for us.

Buck is a good player, an important player. But he isn't competitive unless we prod him. He always expects the worst, and if things don't go well, he sulks and pouts. But when we get him intense or mad, he is virtually unstoppable and scares the living daylights out of opposing teams. They reason that a guy that big has to be a powerful player, and they avoid hitting at him. Opponents usually commit one or two blockers to him, never realizing he isn't that major a part of our offense.

Like a few others on the team, Buck blossomed when Hovland left because he received much more playing time. With more experience, he got better and often dominated the front court in important matches.

Buck's size makes him the center of attention, although he'd prefer to be left alone. He likes to have women notice him, though, and if there are groupies around, they tend to follow Buck. He does indeed stand out in a crowd

Marc Waldie, a 6-4 Ohio Stater from Wichita, Kansas, was the most technically skilled player I have ever coached. I have a great deal of respect for him. Even with all that talent however, he eventually had to accept a backup role when it got closer to the Olympics. Waldie did everything well, but we needed specialists.

His ball handling, blocking, and defense are second to none. He also handles the small details better than anyone. The only characteristics keeping him from being the best in the world are his inability to jump and lack of strength. I doubt he's ever reached a 30-inch vertical jump. But boy, is he skilled.

When he first joined the National team—he joined in 1976 and was in Dayton the entire time we were there—I thought he fought every decision I made. He realized he was more talented than anyone else we had, and I think it was tough for him to wait for the others to develop. By the time the Olympics approached, the situation had changed. Injuries and age had become a problem for him, and we had acquired more talented players—the specialists. We no longer needed what Waldie gave us, which was a sound game in all phases of play.

I'll always regret what happened at the World Championships in Argentina in August, 1982. We were working out in Catamarca on a drill I didn't like. We went ahead anyway and everything seemed to go wrong. We were out of sync. We were tired, the floor was dusty, and to continue was an overall bad decision. Waldie was a starter for us then, but he fell and sprained his ankle. Anybody else would have been lost for the entire tournament, but not Waldie. He had our trainer tape over a knot the size of a grapefruit on his ankle, and he played two days later. Eventually, though, he couldn't play and we had to change our rotation.

Waldie was important to us, as much for his stability as for his skills, and after the Outward Bound trip, he was elected captain. He was responsive to our staff and related to us not only his needs, but the team's needs.

When we won the gold medal, Waldie and Berzins embraced first—two non-California kids who had achieved so much in a sport that was so Californian. It was a special moment. Waldie retired after the Olympics.

Chris Marlowe is yet another player from Pacific Palisades. He's 6-4, and he played volleyball and basketball at San Diego State. He is also an actor and volleyball television commentator. Chris was the most charismatic person on the team.

We were teammates on the National Team from 1974 to '76. He quit the team rather than move to Dayton, a decision I didn't like, but respected. He had an acting career to attend to, and he was one of the older players. At the Los Angeles Games, he was just short of 33 years old.

In the spring of 1982, Marlowe asked if he could rejoin the team. I never expected him to come out of retirement, but he felt he could help us, and he wanted to play. Ordinarily, I would have said no. Marlowe hadn't played competitively for five years, but he also hadn't joined the pro league. I have strong feelings about that. If we were going to have a team, we couldn't allow players to drop off to play for pay, then drop back on the roster when they felt like it, while others were committed to the team all along. Marlowe demonstrated a commitment to the national program, or at least the sport.

Marlowe raised the intensity level at practice, and that helped us develop at a more rapid rate. Chris was not a highly skilled volleyball player, and was well past his prime, but he could get the most out of our team. He's a fun-loving guy, the kind of volleyball player who plays because he enjoys it. If anyone on our team deserved to be called a winner, it was Marlowe.

Over the years, we had many great players join the team, and 12 spots don't allow for much leeway. Eventually, we had to cut Marlowe.

That was the most difficult decision I had to make during my tenure as National coach.

Another setter, Rod Wilde had just beaten out Marlowe. For a long time, the other coaches and I went back and forth, Rod or Chris. If we had taken a team vote, Marlowe would have stayed because of his popularity, but we had to make a decision based on more than friendship.

Marlowe took it better than anybody on the team. He shook hands and said he thought we were making a mistake, but accepted our decision. It was the only time during my four years with the team in San Diego that I was close to tears. Chris Marlowe is quite a man. I have more respect for him than for anybody else I've ever coached.

Two months later, Wilde broke his ankle and we asked Marlowe back. The other players welcomed him and elected him captain just before the Olympics, soon after he rejoined the team.

Marlowe only disappointed me once. Before our match against Tunisia, I told him that he would be our water and towel guy because it wasn't clear whether the trainer would be allowed on the court. Marlowe's one of the most unselfish players on the team, but he argued with me over that chore.

"I'm not going to carry water out there," Marlowe said.

"You'll do it," I said.

"That's not a job for a player," he said. "Especially a captain."

The rest of the conversation was nasty. It might have been the way I presented my case, but our conversation got out of hand. We argued before, during, and after the match, and I never did get around to telling him of another reason I wanted him in our timeout huddles. I thought he would be a calming influence if he huddled with the team even though he wasn't playing.

As it turned out, the trainer was allowed out, and Marlowe didn't have to disobey my orders. Still, it was a good thing we were playing Tunisia and not Korea!

Aldis Berzins, from Kennett Square, Pennsylvania, near Philadelphia, is our unsung hero. He has a soccer background, and at 6-2 is very quick. He is polite, quiet, and well mannered, and he doesn't fluster in the wake of criticism. When other players yell at him to get rid of frustrations, Berzins never retaliates. He soaks up all their frustrations, smiles, then goes on to play terrific ball.

Berzins is worth so much more than his athletic ability, although he is outstanding at passing and on defense. He has an incredible ability to control hard-hit spikes and is our number one serve receiver. Always in the right spot, he can play balls from the most unusual body positions, and has saved more balls with one arm than most players control with two.

Berzins' backcourt play is phenomenal and keeps getting better. He and our system fit like they were made for each other. He and Karch Kiraly own the backcourt. They hardly ever talk back there; they don't seem to have to. Almost any coach will insist passing is the most important part of the game and must be practiced the most, but we never worry about it. Aldis and Karch know where each other will be at all times.

It annoyed me that the media didn't want to talk to him when they asked for special interviews. He is a fabulous player. I probably shouldn't fault the media for that one, though. I never felt Berzins would be a starter when he joined the team in the summer of 1977. I felt he was limited by his size and jumping ability. His hitting percentages were terrible through 1980 and 1981.

He finally became a starter in the summer of 1983, and from that time on, we improved dramatically. He was a major player on the drive to the gold medal.

Pat Powers, like Sunderland, is from Malibu, and is our third USC graduate. He has had a very interesting career. At 6-5, he is an imposing player with great jumping ability; but in 1981, the year after he joined us, he was on and off. He wasn't really good enough to be with us then, but we saw something that made us think that with training and maturity, he would add significantly to his skills. Eventually, he did mature.

He was irresponsible in those early days. While we were playing in the Canada Cup in Winnipeg, I was going to sub him, but couldn't find him. Finally, someone told me he was in another part of the arena shooting baskets!

We released Powers after that tournament, but told him we wanted to look at him again in about a year when he might be ready for us. He thought we were nuts. But he kept working and didn't leave San Diego. We gave him that other chance after the World Championships of 1982.

Actually, Pat's one of the more enjoyable players on our team. Because he listens. He tries. He works at making changes to improve his skills.

Powers was never a full-time starter, but he was usually on the floor when the team was playing its best. He's one of those guys who puts a lot of pressure on himself, so we've had to use him cautiously. We benched him after our Argentina match in the Olympics and got him to see how the team could play without him. When we finally put him back in during the middle of the first Brazil pool match, he played beautifully. He was probably our best hitter the rest of the Olympics — tremendous on the outside.

He gets frustrated from time to time, but generally he's coachable, and not a selfish player at all.

Karch Kiraly, from Santa Barbara, is our best player. He is a 6-3 UCLA graduate. He was probably the most publicized athlete in the history of volleyball from the time he was a sophomore in high school. Yet in the Olympics, he was a shadow of what he could be. I don't know if the pressure got to him, or if he recognized the team didn't need to rely on him.

He's talented in everything he does. I suspect he will become the finest volleyball player ever in this country. There really isn't anything he can't do. Only his size will restrict his eventual impact on the game. He's one of the best jumpers and strongest athletes I've ever seen, and he's able to listen to advice and immediately go out on the court and perform. He can integrate movement patterns mentally without rehersal. That's a very rare trait.

Kiraly began playing with us just after our Brazil tour in 1981. He started as a setter, but could play almost any position. He's a capable and versatile player and has the ability to lift a team's performance level by sheer willpower and ability.

He's had to struggle with his temper and inner drive. He isn't an easy guy to know. He is uncommunicative and stays by himself. No one really knows Karch very well. In practice, he's a demon, going full out all the time.

The chance to coach someone like that doesn't happen very often. He allows us to run so many systems, we can maximize other player's skills because of him. He has made plays nobody else in the world could make, yet he's never happy with his performance.

In the end, at the Games, we weren't happy with his performance either, but maybe it's because we know what he can do at the top of his game.

Two other players certainly deserve special recognition. Many players who did not reach the final cut helped make up this team. They all contributed in some way. The last two who left our squad contributed more, and it hurt not having them out there in uniform when we won the gold medal.

Rod Wilde is from Iowa and went to college at Pepperdine. He was one of those guys who joined us after playing pro volleyball, which folded. When he regained his amateur status, he came to us in the summer of 1982.

Wilde is high strung, very emotional, and intense. He is also very open and honest and wants to be liked by everybody.

Easy to coach, he's willing to do anything. He's a great setter with tremendous range. He could chase down bad passes better than anyone else I've ever seen. He earned his spot on the team under the most difficult of circumstances. Not only was he not well liked by the other players, but the player we cut in his place, Marlowe, was the most liked. It was a difficult situation to deal with, but it didn't seem to affect Rod's play. He is a wonderful guy.

We never were able to integrate him into the team, though. On the court, he tried to do everything, and after a while, the other guys would say, "Okay, you do it." They thought he was a hot dog, but he wasn't. He just tried to help the best he could.

Then, on May 13, in the last game of the last match against the Soviets in Kharkov, Ukraine, Wilde broke his leg. One of the Soviet Union's best players went out of control and fell under the net. Rod fell over him.

As I ran onto the court, I knew it was serious. Rod had two broken bones in his leg, and the pain must have been excruciating. Yet he said to me, "Thank God it wasn't Dvorak."

Imagine that. Here's a guy whose dream is crushed, yet he's grateful he was hurt instead of a player the team was counting on more.

The other players were sympathetic, but I'm sure they were glad it wasn't them.

It was only about two months to the Olympics. Wilde thought he could be ready to play, but I knew he wouldn't. He was great through it all. His spirit shone brightly. At the Olympics, he was an alternate.

The last player we cut, and the other Olympic alternate, was Mike Blanchard. He, too, was tough to let go. I must admit to an empty feeling when he left after being with the team for four years and playing in every competition. By that time, though, I had my mind more on the Games themselves than on this man's broken dreams. But he took it well.

Over the previous year, I had talked with Mike, trying to warn him his spot on the team was not secure. When we cut Marlowe, we took Blanchard aside.

"You know, this could happen to you, too," I said.

"I know. Tell me, what do I have to do to make it?" he said.

What could I tell him? Become someone else?

It wasn't a piece of cake to cut Blanchard. It wasn't really fair to him, after all he had done. But he was a victim of the system. You don't take the best 12 players for a team; you look for the 12 best role players. We simply didn't have a role for him.

He had given me less concern than anyone on the team and it was a pitiful way to reward a guy for that. But it had to be done. We just couldn't keep everybody.

Blanchard was another player who had been with me on the Junior Olympic team in 1976, and was with the National team since 1981. He always did what we wanted. He always asked if he could do more. He was the type of guy a person would want as a lifelong friend.

At the Olympics, we had to put our best team on the floor and sometimes the nicest people don't always make the best players. Blanchard couldn't beat out anyone ahead of him, and we needed to cut one man.

I'm pretty sure Blanchard knew by the time the cut was made that he would be the guy to go.

I imagine the worst thing for Wilde and Blanchard to do was go to the Olympics and sit in a seat watching the U.S. team play. It was particularly trying for Blanchard. He hadn't missed a single competition in the four years we were in San Diego, and now he would miss the biggest one of all.

People never hear about the guys who play lesser roles, but those two played as big a part as anybody, and they never walked onto the floor at Long Beach.

Without them, without the hundreds of others who tried out, who pushed us, who prodded, we would not have been the team we were, and the United States would not have won the gold medal.

Perhaps this is too emotional, too much hype and too much criticism of players who won a gold medal for the United States. Some of it is. But from my perspective, there wasn't a man on the team who didn't contribute greatly to our effort, and there were many more who didn't make the team but made contributions that will never be fully acknowledged.

Those people deserve credit, for they took time out of their normal lives to help the United States win the gold medal. I am proud of each and every one of them.

Chapter 4.

U.S. volleyball: the sad past.

Reaching, and winning, the gold medal match at the 1984 Los Angeles Olympics obviously didn't just happen for the team. The course was carefully plotted for many years, although it wasn't always smooth. Several times it looked like we didn't have a program at all, in spite of our careful plans.

Not many people know this, but volleyball was invented in this country. A fellow named William G. Morgan was playing around at a YMCA in Holyoke, Massachusetts, way back in 1895, when he developed the game. This was shortly after basketball was invented down the road in Springfield.

Yet it wasn't until 1949 that the first World Volleyball Championship was held. The United States did not even enter. In 1964, volleyball became an Olympic sport. The United States finished ninth in Tokyo. In 1968, we finished seventh in Mexico City. We didn't qualify again until 1984.

That's 16 years in which the country of origin couldn't qualify. For a country this size, that's embarrassing.

There were many reasons for our mediocrity. Most stemmed from the lack of organization needed to create quality players. There really wasn't a program at all in those early days. Each year a new National Team was chosen and began training around June. If a player had made the team before, he probably had some advantage; but basically players had to try out again, year after year.

Not only that, but each year a new coach was chosen to put the team together, and never early enough to formulate any long-range plans. It was much like the way college football runs its all-star games for seniors, except that all-star games are played between teams in similar situations and are essentially set up so players can impress pro scouts.

In individual sports, such as track, an athlete can compete around the world on his own. In a team sport like basketball, thousands of qualified players are involved with highly competitive college teams during the year. In volleyball, things are different. Not many colleges have volleyball teams that train players for international competition, and most are located in the west, primarily in California. We just don't have the player base basketball has.

My first involvement with the national volleyball program came in the spring of 1969. Two of my Ohio State volleyball teammates and I drove to California during spring break and had the opportunity to train with an international team. The team was on its way to a tournament in South America; that was the first time I realized I might be able to play for the National Team.

But the program was disorganized and haphazard. Virtually anybody who had any ability could go to a practice. Here these guys were a team, and three college students from Ohio State stopped by, and not only trained with them, but actually played in a couple of tuneup matches. Most of the players who went on that trip were 1968 Olympians who had only trained for a month at most. That's an indication of how unstructured the program was.

National programs had always been run that way, and they wouldn't change for almost 10 more years.

After I graduated from Ohio State in 1970, I was invited by Jim Coleman, the U.S. coach, to try out for the National Team that was going to play in the World Championships.

Coleman, one of the few serious volleyball coaches, had coached the 1968 Olympic team and was one of the few people in this country who was dedicated to being a great coach. He really studied the international game.

Anyway, I went out to California and trained for what I considered an awfully long time, 10 weeks. Most of the established players decided not to play that year. They had good reason. Players had to pay their own expenses. There was no per diem or housing. The players had to make do for themselves.

A couple of friends and I found an apartment in Inglewood. I moved two or three times that summer while we were in training. We got to know the Los Angeles area well. But the only strategy I learned was how to get off the Hollywood Freeway — there was no effective training program.

So who tried out for the team? Maybe a hundred different players came to practice, most of them playing for no more than a week or two. We trained in the evening sometimes, in the morning sometimes, and sometimes on weekends. We trained whenever the coaches could get free, and when most of the players weren't working.

We tried to embark on a new program in 1970. That wasn't revolutionary. The USVBA was always trying to embark on a new program.

It was somewhat less than ideal. I made the team and played on a national team for most of the next six years. What made me stay was my love of the game, the travel, the overall experience. I wanted to be part of something that could get better. I dreamed and talked of a gold medal even then, but only briefly.

This is what usually happened: We'd go to a competition, perform to the height of our mediocrity and return to wherever we came from. Then we'd wait until the following summer and try it all over again.

Dreaming and talking is about all we did. We didn't know how to work for what we wanted.

What a frustrating situation! The coaches and players were never happy with the way things were going. But there appeared to be no other way to do things.

The money was limited — only what the U.S. Olympic Committee granted the Volleyball Association. There was little effort at outside fund-raising. We had no corporate contracts, no community support, no home for the National Team. It was just a bunch of guys gathering in one location trying to find cheap apartments for the summer.

To expect any kind of success was ridiculous. You get what you pay into a program.

Yet sometimes our expectations rose. We did have good talent and we occasionally won a match against a strong opponent. More frequently, however, we lost matches to inferior teams. I remember losing to Tunisia in 1970, and I don't think they had a player over six feet tall. We lost to France, and they had less than a marginal team.

Some of us can laugh at that now, although most of us won't admit we participated in those matches. I usually hear, "No, I was on the bench. It wasn't my fault we lost." We were bad, and at times embarrassing.

By 1972, we had finally put together a good team; probably the best the United States had until 1984. Yet at the Olympic final qualifier in Montpellier, France, we lost a discouraging five-game match to Poland. We just didn't have the consistency, or the confidence in each other, or the level of training, to win under difficult circumstances.

None of that meant much, however. In 1973 only 13 players tried out, some of them still in high school. We did have one of those unusual victories though, that are difficult to explain. We beat Cuba three straight in the finals of the Zone Championships and qualified for the World Cup. We wouldn't beat Cuba again until 1981.

The Zones are held every two years. The first Zone following an Olympic year qualifies a team for the World Cup and World Championships. The second Zone qualifies a team for the next Olympics.

In 1973, we also beat Brazil and Bulgaria, at the World Cup in Czechoslovakia. That may have been the high point of our season.

We toured Europe and Japan in 1974, only to be crushed by the Soviet Union and Poland, and then by a Korean team for 13th place in the World Championships. It was discouraging to say the least.

The following year, we actually beat Czechoslovakia. But in the Zone Championships, we lost not only to Cuba, but also to Mexico.

Many of the players who had been playing for five years quit after the Zones in August of 1975. Those who had developed themselves into valuable players were no longer available. So we nearly had to start over. There were also a few rumblings that McGown should be removed as coach. I would hear that again several years later.

Again, there was minimal training, no real experience, and heartbreak. We lost a match to Brazil in the Pan American Games that we should have won. It wouldn't be the last time we would see Brazil, or some of that team's great players. Bernard Rajzman, who played in 1984, and Paulo Roberto Freitas, who was the 1984 coach, both played against us in 1975.

That same year, we had an interesting series of five matches against the Soviet Union. We were plastered in each match, of course, and won only two games. That's two games, not two matches. One of the games we won, ironically, was in Dayton while we were testing it out as our possible future home.

Yuri Chesnekov, the Soviet coach, was a father figure to us. McGown and I went to his room after the matches and he acted like he was teaching his son how to drive. He spoke broken English through an interpreter, and scattered diagrams and charts all over the room for us.

"You can no play like that," Chesnekov sputtered. "Why do these things? You can no do it."

"But this is the way we learned how to block," I said.

"No, no, no," he said. "This way. And train this way. And serve this way." And on and on.

The guy felt sorry for us.

We advanced because we learned his lessons and some new ones of our own.

When we won the gold medal, Chesnekov was there behind us in his blue officials' blazer. I turned and flashed two fingers, for victory and for two passers. We were able to do something our way after all.

We also lost a five-game match to Mexico in the Pan American Games in 1975, and, to Cuba again in three straight. Early in 1976, we lost in an Olympic-qualifying tournament to Yugoslavia, a mediocre team.

Obviously a pattern was developing. Good intentions, hope, frustration, then despair. But, a few significant changes were being made that would be the guide for what we would do in the future.

In 1973, the USVBA made a long-range move by hiring McGown for four seasons. They made a commitment to continuity, and it was a meaningful move. Unfortunately, that was about all they could do then. There still was no budget, no staff, no permanent training facility. The best McGown could hope for was that the players would gather themselves on their own, work out, and train when they could get free. Every spring McGown would either go to California, where most of the players were, or invite them to Brigham Young University where he taught, and work out a training schedule. In the fall, it would all be over. It wasn't much compared with what the Europeans were doing, but it was a step in the right direction.

The women's team was working on several major improvements, and in 1975, a full-time National coach, Arie Selinger, was hired. The women's team began year-round training at a center in Pasadena, Texas, a suburb of Houston. That was a most significant move by the association. While it didn't pay immediate dividends, it would eventually be tried for the men, and it led to our success.

One of the most important issues for the USVBA and the men's team came out of the formation of that women's training center. The whole history of the men's team, the gold medal future, hinged on how the association perceived the center's success.

Later that year, the women's team played in the National Championships and performed horribly. The association had given the women's team a home, a full-time coach and backing, and had nothing to show for its effort.

Al Monaco of the USVBA stood behind the women's program, even after the poor showings at the National Championships and later that year at the Pan American Games final Olympic Qualifying Tournament.To accept that, to go on from there, was a rare, longsighted decision that eventually paid off. It was a badly needed vote of confidence. We stayed with the training center approach, and volleyball in this country was on its way.

I would like to think I had something to do with the eventual decision to stick with that concept, but Monaco, McGown, and others certainly stood up for the training center, too.

Once it was established, we tried to decide on a training schedule for the women, the competition the team would need, and other details that would also be used later for the men.

The next job was to open a training center for the men, and officials were looking for a suitable place for us to begin that mission.

Chapter 5.

Dayton, Ohio.
Where the snowdrifts are.

Cities didn't clamor for us to join their communities as they might have for a major league baseball team.

We got offers from cities that wanted to be the home for the men's team but couldn't fulfill our needs. Although the men's team had never had any real success, some cities thought it might be an honor to host a National Team. Some looked upon us as a publicity stunt.

Most cities had no idea of what hosting a team would involve. They didn't realize it takes lots of work as well as commitment — by individuals and businesses alike.

It happened that the first proposal to the USVBA came from Dayton, during the USVBA Championships in May, 1975. Frank Gunn, a Dayton resident and volleyball enthusiast, was involved in a local junior program. At a clinic in Toronto he discussed the problem of our national team's disappointing performance history with a number of successul foreign coaches who felt this country didn't take the game seriously. After all, we didn't train, pay our coaches, or provide experience for our players. So Gunn went back to Dayton with an idea; he hounded the Dayton Chamber of Commerce and other interested groups, with the glitter of operating a National Training Center.

It took more than a year and a half, but Dayton became the official training center of the U.S. Men's National Volleyball Team in January, 1977.

What a winter that was.

I was hired as National coach in December, 1976, in Los Angeles. I made it to Dayton during one of the worst blizzards in the history of the Midwest.

That didn't bother me; I was used to such weather. But most of our players would be Californians, and I wondered how they would take the weather conditions. As it turned out, my doubts were legitimate — snowshoes and volleyball just don't mix.

Players began arriving in Dayton in February, 1977. The Californians didn't have a clue as to how to deal with or live in a Midwestern city blanketed by one of the worst snowfalls ever.

Two of those players — Ralph Smith and Joe Battalia — drove cross-country in Joe's ancient Volkswagon bug. They arrived in Dayton wearing every piece of clothing they owned to fend off the cold. Naturally, they looked bewildered and lost.

We got them warm and settled into an apartment. They started training and eventually found work loading railroad cars at the White Villa Foods warehouse. It was pretty tough to see a gold medal glinting in those early days.

The training center was to involve the best players in the country, based on ability. We never wanted to eliminate a player for reasons that might be within our control, such as jobs, schooling, or family. We wanted players to make the team because they were good enough, not because they were available, and we didn't want to lose the best players because they couldn't afford to be members of the team.

This wasn't to be a charity program, however. Players were expected to work and train. We initiated an Olympic Jobs Opportunity Program but that met with minimal success. We secured the jobs, but not as quickly as had been anticipated. Even now, we'd like to come up with the jobs before the players arrive, but we haven't yet figured out a way to accomplish that in every case.

The U.S. Olympic Committee had promised cooperation, but they hardly helped at all. Most of what we accomplished we did on our own, which made us wonder what the USOC officials meant when they were quoted about their help in rounding up jobs for their athletes. Some of the jobs they were so proud of belonged to volleyball players, and we were the ones responsible for those. This annoyed Cliff McPeak, who was in charge of the physical education program at Wright State University, where we set up our operation. McPeak would later take a job with the USVBA and is most responsible for our corporate sponsorships and general fundraising. In Dayton, along with the Dayton Volleyball Association — a small support group — and several businesses, he did all he could and helped us more than anyone else.

Our program was different than that of the women's team's training center, even though theirs started before ours did. Their only job was to practice every day. We wanted our players to be the best possible volleyball players, but also wanted to prepare them for their future and give them job opportunities. We wanted them to grow in a number of directions and thought our philosophy would culminate in better, more dedicated, and mature athletes.

That philosophy helped us later. We had a team able to deal with a complex system, make adjustments, and handle adversity. They were not simply single-minded automatons, machines that played volleyball, but were responsible young people in a multifaceted program.

Sunderland joined us, along with a few other players who ultimately did not make the team. Tom Ashen was one. Ashen became Director of Competition for the 1984 Olympic Games, and worked for the Los Angeles Olympic Committee running the venue for volleyball at the Long Beach Arena.

Mike Cote, a future architect, played, and Fred Sturm, who later became head men's and women's coach at Stanford. We also had Tim Lawler, a future lawyer, Ted Dodd, and Duwelius. Most weren't great volleyball players, they were great people.

Not all of them remained with the team, for various reasons, but they all were part of us and part of our final success.

Our first players in Dayton worked during the day and practiced at night, from 7-10 p.m., in Roosevelt Center. The gymnasium was on the top floor, had a low ceiling, and only one court. It was poorly lit and poorly maintained. We had humble beginnings. One night we were even locked in, and had to wait for a custodian to let us out.

Later, we changed our practice courts to Wright State University and Sinclair Community College.

Another factor began to bother me. I was thrilled to have the opportunity to coach the National Team. But I began to think of how young I was, and how little experience I had as a coach in the international game!

Certainly I had been around volleyball a long time and had participated with the National Team for a number of years. Yet I was only 29 years old, and had only a few years of coaching experience.

It must have been a dilemma for the USVBA, too. I don't know if they really wanted me, but I met enough of their requirements to apply. I was single, could relocate easily, and could accept the salary of about $12,000 for coaching and teaching at Wright State University. Others might have needed more money.

But no one discussed the fact that I was singularly unprepared to be a national coach and lead a team to an Olympics.

Much of what I felt and knew about coaching came from Carl McGown, a man I greatly respect and admire. However, to have a successful program, I felt we had to push and train players harder and move the team beyond where Carl had taken it.

That's probably the hallmark of a young coach or teacher. I wanted the people under me to go far beyond where I had ever gone. I wanted to push them farther than I had ever been pushed.

In the back of my mind I had the idea that I had worked pretty hard as a player and was both determined and dedicated. Also, since I was young, I went out of my way to be authoritarian, inflexible, and arrogant. Some people say I never relinquished those traits.

I still have strong emotions regarding the concept of success. Success goes beyond winning and losing to the realization of a goal. I can understand how

Rick Carey felt when he won the gold medal in swimming, but was unhappy with his time. People thought he was a fool for feeling that way, but he was young and had worked hard to be the best in his field, and he fell short of his personal goal.

Sometimes, winning isn't enough. Sometimes a person can lose while still reaching the highest obtainable level. That too is success.

With hindsight, I can see we were doomed from the start in Dayton, not only because of the location, but because of my inexperience at the time.

Still, our goal was to reach the Olympic Games, and we were on the right path.

The Olympics involves 10 teams chosen in various ways. The host team is invited automatically, as is the winner of the previous Olympics. That means the day the Olympics end, two teams are already qualified for the next Olympics. The USA and Korea are qualified for Seoul, Korea, in 1988. (That has a nice ring to it, doesn't it?)

Five other teams are chosen from five Zones around the world: the African, European, Asian, and South American Zones, and collectively, the North American, Central American and Carribean Zone, of which the United States is a part. Abbreviated, ours is the NORCECA Zone.

Qualification matches in the Zones are usually held a year prior to the Olympics. In case a team wins, but has already qualified, say, as the host team, the second place team in the Zone gets the Olympic bid.

Two years after the Olympics, the next qualifying tournament is held, the World Championships. One team is chosen from that field. Finally, there is a special tournament in January of the Olympic year for all previous nonqualifiers. The top two teams from that tournament normally complete the Olympic field.

For the Los Angeles Games, that format changed slightly. Instead of two teams being selected from the last tournament, only one was chosen. The last Olympic qualifier came from the World Cup Tournament, held the year after the 1980 Moscow Olympic Games. For 1984, we actually qualified twice, as the host team and Zone champion. We felt we had to win that Zone championship in Indianapolis so no one could say we backed into the Olympics only as the host team.

At any rate, during the Dayton years, we competed in all the major tournaments as well as several smaller ones and on several exhibition tours. We were dismal.

In 1977, about nine months after starting in Dayton, we received a special invitation to play in the World Cup Tournament in Japan. It wasn't a qualifying tournament, but a team had to be good to be there, and we weren't. Yugoslavia had dropped out at the last minute. We were in Winnipeg for the Canada Cup Tournament at the time, finishing third out of four teams. The only team we beat was made up of ex-Canadian National players. Al Monaco called from the USVBA office and asked if we could have a team ready to go to Japan in about four days.

Yes, and we'd like to be the first team to train on the moon, too.

Four weeks wouldn't have been enough time, or four months. Later we realized we needed four years, but it was an invitation we couldn't refuse. We found out graphically how far we had to go to become world class.

Before we went, I telephoned a few good college players to see if they could help us out. I got Bob Yoder from USC, Dave Olbright from UCLA, Nester Pazlowski from Rutgers, and a backcourt phenom from Ohio State named Aldis Berzins.

Those four joined the players already on the roster and gathered in San Fransisco for one quick practice session before we flew to Japan.

We expected what happened. "Annihilated" almost describes it. Brazil and Japan cleaned us out. We did beat Canada and Egypt, so we finished about tenth. But we were clearly not a world caliber team. It was a good experience though, since it was our first crack at a semiqualifying tournament.

There was an interesting combination of players on that team. Four — Sunderland, Duwelius, Waldie, and Berzins — stayed to be members of the gold medal team. Several others went on to become coaches, including Yoder, Olbright, Scott Nelson, and Gerry Gregory.

So we developed more than just good volleyball players. We also developed careers.

In 1978 we went to the World Championships in Ancona, Italy, for our first real qualifying tournament. There were 24 teams, broken down into six, four-team pools. Each of the pools played a round-robin, and the top two teams from those pools continued in another round-robin inside each of two six-team pools for places 1-12. The bottom two in each pool went for places 13-24 in the same way.

That was a lot of volleyball to be played, and the key was placement in the first pool. It was no good being one of the top five or six teams in the world if the initial pool included three teams that were obviously better. To lose badly in the first pool meant no chance to show a true world-wide standing.

It would be similar, say, to a second place team in the National League having a better record than the first place team in the American League, yet not getting a chance to play in the World Series.

We certainly didn't have to worry about that, but our first pairing, unfortunately, was not very advantageous. We played in a group with Rumania, Czechoslovakia, and Korea, each a very difficult, highly ranked opponent.

And we lost to all three, by 3-0 scores.

Right from the start we couldn't finish in the top 12 of the tournament, and would not qualify there for the Olympics. Still, we had to continue playing and found ourselves in a group with Finland, Venezuela, Argentina, Hungary, and Rumania.

We beat Hungary, Argentina, and Venezuela, but lost to Finland after being up two games to none! And we couldn't play Rumania again because we carried our loss over from the first pool.

We finished third in that group of six and then had the humiliating opportunity to play off for places 17 through 20.

We went right out and lost to Belgium, 3-0. That loss, coupled with the loss to Finland, were easily two of the lowest points of my coaching career. The next day, we beat Canada for a rather inglorious 19th place finish. About the best thing to come out of the tournament, besides experience, was our chance to see Venice, one of the world's most beautiful cities.

It was after that ordeal that I made the decision to return to playing and give up coaching.

Our second qualifying opportunity came at the Zone matches in Cuba during the spring of 1979. We left Dayton to do some final training in Miami and thought, optimistically, that we had a chance of qualifying — more the eternal optimism of the American athlete than any realism, given our team and the ability of the Cubans.

We were promptly blown away. We were completely disorganized and not only did we lose to the Cubans, but we lost to a team from the Dominican Republic as well.

As if we hadn't learned enough in Cuba, we went on to Bulgaria in January 1980, for our last attempt at qualifying. There were rumors of a boycott, and the United States did announce its boycott shortly after that tournament, but we went thinking we would qualify.

The Bulgarian tournament caused controversy inside the ranks when several college players — specifically Sinjin Smith, Tim Hovland, Dusty Dvorak, and Pat Powers — were enlisted to beef up the team.

Adding those young players created bitter and mixed feelings. The guys who had been with the program in Dayton desperately wanted to win. They knew the new players had outstanding talents and would help, but on the other hand, they had a tough time accepting them since none of them had invested in our program. The new guys, all from California, began making derogatory statements about the effectiveness of the Dayton program, some of our players, and even the coaches. A rift developed between the new players and the Dayton players.

We played well with this "mixed" team, but still lost to Bulgaria and Korea. Bulgaria and Rumania qualified from that tournament. Those two teams later became medalists behind the Soviets at the Olympics that year.

Although the tournament ended our Olympic dream — some of the sting was taken out later when we learned about the boycott — our team had shown it could compete. I realized then we had the makings of a special team.

It excited me to see the talents of those younger players, although I chafed at the unpleasant experience they had with our "Dayton team." As a group they seemed to have enormous egos, were lazy, and generally resisted coaching — attributes that made the challenge harder. But I was more determined than ever to mold a championship team.

It was then I decided what I really wanted to do was coach the team again, and I realized any real chance at success would have to come from a venue outside of Dayton.

The problems of the Dayton program are easy to detail. It simply was the wrong place to train a volleyball team in the United States. Volleyball has just recently been popularized outside of California and only because of our Olympic victory and the emergence of women's sports. It is essentially a southern Californian sport.

Also, Dayton is a typical Midwestern city that was going through difficult times. A number of corporations had either pulled out of town or closed their doors. It was nearly impossible to assimilate 10 to 15 young men into that job market. Dayton, though it tried hard, was just unable to help.

It's also a very tradition-oriented city, conservative, and different from the environment of the average player we were trying to attract. And that doesn't even address the weather conditions. We had players leave us who simply could not handle the cold and snow. These were guys who went surfing in their spare time, not cross-country skiing.

Yet as I look back, the hearts in Dayton were in the right place. It was a novel idea and we wanted to benefit the city as much as we hoped to benefit ourselves.

McPeak left Wright State University in 1979 and joined the USVBA full time in Colorado. If we gained nothing else from Dayton, we got a fantastic employee who has done more than anyone to professionalize our national association. McPeak was the real guiding light and soul of the training center in San Diego from 1980 through '84.

I still remain in contact with Pat Crawford, who helped as our secretary in addition to her other responsibilities at Wright State. It seems we had to borrow from everyone in Dayton. Our office was a room about eight feet square and our equipment was stored in two large filing cabinets along the wall.

Don Mohr, the WSU athletic director, would stop by frequently to lend his special kind of upbeat support. He gave lots of himself and his time.

In spite of our many problems, the people of Dayton were great to us. We were simply too far from the talent pool, and very far from spectator support.

We did have our moments, though. A volleyball magazine published in Santa Barbara, California, the only one of its kind then, used to take us apart pretty good. A general feeling evolved, fueled by this publication, that our National Team couldn't even beat a good college team. Then in late 1978, we invited USC, one of the best college teams, to a series of matches to help our training. USC had a great team that featured Powers, Dvorak, and Hovland.

The players on that team thought they'd come in and romp us. We won every match.

That was a lesson for me as well as the detractors. It showed readily what kind of effect year-round training can have on even less talented athletes. It was a satisfying experience for the players and the coaches. Our program, for all its faults, was working.

It was obvious we had to move, though. After a while, it was decided to find a new site, which was fine for the people of Dayton as well. They weren't exactly tugging at our shirt tails to keep us there. We kept asking for more than they could provide.

Yet that was where we got our start, and I shall always be indebted to Dayton for that.

Chapter 6.

San Diego.
Sunshine at last.

The U.S. National Volleyball team had to find a new home. San Diego seemed a perfect choice.

First, the year-round climate was more suitable. San Diego had better facilities, and the job opportunities for the players were greater. Last, and most important, we would be in southern California, the largest source of players.

If the training center program was to work at all, it would work in San Diego. We made the move in January, 1981.

All wasn't perfect in San Diego, of course. We had our problems, including some similar to ones we encountered in Dayton. But we stayed with it.

The training center was the only way we could compete, although a lot of people told me the training center concept is socialistic or Eastern European, almost like communism.

I really resent that kind of talk. In the first place, if athletes are going to enter international competition, they ought to enter to win. Competition isn't there just for the experience. Nice experiences can be found on vacations, where no work has to be done. Our training center is an integral part of our motivation to win. Those who think we copy the East Europeans are very naive about what it takes to be successful on this level. They don't understand our program or the European program.

We did copy some elements of the European system, but we adapted them creatively into an American system. We don't force people to be involved, which is a major difference between us and the East Europeans. Our players also have the responsibility of holding a job or attending school — some do both — in addition to their work on the volleyball courts.

That's quite different from the facade the East Europeans use. The players over there are simply there to play volleyball or ice hockey or some other sport. They are not expected, or even allowed, to be responsible for the rest of their lives.

At the start, we needed an autocratic program dominated by a very strong figure, and I was certainly willing to take on that responsibility.

We needed to create an environment, a training center, where the players are together year-round. Before we began, we set a minimum of 50 international matches a year for our players so they would be ready to compete in the major tournaments.

We needed to put several thousand hours a year into the gym, not a couple hundred hours. We needed a year-round weight and physical training program, and a sports medicine program to evaluate what kind of performance level the players could maintain. We needed to prepare, and prepare systematically. Period.

We looked for a total environment, too, where the players could work, play, and train. That's what we strove for, and we were successful in setting up that structure even if all parts of it didn't work to our satisfaction immediately.

So we created a program designed to meet those needs and settled in San Diego, despite our detractors who didn't want a program like ours in *any* location.

Although San Diego was more suitable overall than Dayton, volleyball players didn't drop out of the trees to join us. In many respects, our lack of success in Dayton haunted us when we finally moved to San Diego in January, 1981.

When we decided to look around for a new location, we were convinced it had to be a west-coast community, one that had some knowledge of volleyball, and we preferred southern California. Cliff McPeak put together a 50-page outline on what a community would have to provide for us. He contacted some chambers of commerce as well as selected individuals.

Two major communities were interested — San Diego and Long Beach. The interest in Long Beach came mainly through Dick Carlson, a volleyball enthusiast who sponsored a local club team. His son played too, and they were close to a number of the National players who had been members of his Long Beach team. However, San Diego seemed more interested in having us and offered more facilities.

Donald Sammis, a real estate developer and former pro league owner of the team Neville coached, was the main mover behind that proposal.

McPeak, Monaco, and I spoke with Sammis, and we were impressed. He offered us free office space, some dollars to work with, and the promise of help with our jobs program.

Once we moved, we grew quickly. We were a risky and heretofore unsuccessful team, yet Sammis started us off with more than $50,000, an enormous contribution for one man to make. We ended up with an annual budget of nearly $500,000 before the quadrennial ended. Most of this we had to generate ourselves.

But Sammis gave us the confidence we needed, too. Don sold us on his enthusiasm, the players were excited about relocating in San Diego, we had office space, we were told the community would support us, and we were ready to roll.

For practice, we were given time in the Federal Building, a public gymnasium on the Balboa Park grounds near the famous San Diego Zoo. It's a city gym, and it seemed as though every activity imaginable occurred in the place. It was also a home to most of the park's vagrants and transients.

San Diego has nearly perfect daily weather, so the Federal Building is neither heated nor air conditioned. But the perfect weather is outdoors. When we practiced on winter mornings, the place felt cold enough to keep ice cream in our lunch boxes. In the summer, it was so hot we spent most of our time mopping perspiration off the floor.

And, as usual, the ceiling was just a little bit low, although we made do.

There was also the Great Lost Equipment Caper. We kept our equipment and uniforms locked in a room inside the building, but for a period of a couple months, our stuff kept disappearing. We changed the locks on the doors, set up trip wires and all kinds of gizmos, but the police could never find out who was getting in, or how.

We saw kids around the gym wearing our uniforms that they'd bought at flea markets.

Finally, the police caught two little guys who had broken in by removing a piece of paneling to the room. They crawled in, took our equipment, and replaced the panel. It was quite an operation.

Until we figured out what was going on, we had to store the equipment in our office. Players would come in from time to time to get new socks or knee pads. It was a real classy operation.

The operation we were most concerned about, though, was our jobs program. It was extremely important to our success. Without it we wouldn't have been able to support our year-round training, staff, and competitive schedule. It was a necessity for our existence.

We needed employers to hire our people — based on their resumes, training, and schooling — but with special, indeed somewhat unique, stipulations. Prospective employers were told our players would be on tour at least three months — total, not consecutive. We requested half-day work, a significant amount of time off for our competitions, and livable salaries. We asked for everything but all the cheese in the moon.

The players liked the idea of the jobs program. It gave them an opportunity to take a break from the grind of practice, and it had long-range benefits beyond the volleyball court.

The jobs program makes the National Training Center unique. We teach self-reliance, and we expect everyone to pull his own weight. We value hard work and don't want players who simply want to vegetate on volleyball to the exclusion of life itself. We want our players to have a broader perspective on their future and to go beyond what is expected of them. We want goal-directed, mature athletes who have ambitions and drive in all aspects of life.

In most cases our program worked and is probably best exemplified by those players who decided to retire after the 1984 Olympics. Three of the four were asked to stay on their jobs, and the fourth, Marlowe, always made it clear he wanted to be an actor, not a banker, which was his job while he was with the team. Sunderland and Duwelius also declined to stay at their jobs, Sunderland to chase a broadcasting career and Duwelius to play volleyball in Italy. Waldie did stay with his company to their mutual satisfaction.

Many of the players didn't understand how difficult it was to secure these jobs, or why they didn't get more money. We were asking those companies for a lot, but we were offering a lot, too. Good athletes are well disciplined. They are loyal to the team effort, and successful businesses work as teams.

When we moved into our new offices, donated by Sammis, the first thing we did was hire Kerry Klostermann, who had been my assistant coach in Dayton. Klostermann had moved back to San Diego, his home, and was working at odds and ends even though he had a doctorate in psychology. I talked him into becoming our general manager and hired a secretary. For several months, it was just the three of us.

Sammis couldn't understand why we needed even that many people. His office was next to ours, and one day he walked in and wanted to know what we were doing. He thought maybe I could have handled all the work we were trying to do.

"Why don't you make a daily log of your projects," Sammis finally said to me one day. "Let me know specifically what you're doing."

I didn't want to take the time to do that, but he was an important sponsor. I certainly didn't want to make him unhappy. So I made out a log, once. I sent it to his office and it either got lost or proved our point. He never asked for another one.

In addition to his benevolence, Sammis came up with a great money-making idea. He and other successful businessmen who had personal tennis courts, lent us their homes and courts so we could throw private parties. We called them the Tennis Court Fund Raisers. For donations by guests, we rigged up a volleyball net and put on private exhibitions against some of the foreign teams we traveled with. It was a great idea, and we made $15-25,000 with each one.

Even though Sammis thought we didn't need it, I had to hire an assistant coach, and Neville was my only real choice. In fact, when we both applied for the head job in San Diego, we made a pact of sorts. The guy who got the job would hire the one who didn't. Hiring Bill Neville was the single best decision I made in the years leading up to the Olympics.

It was up to us to assemble the rest of the team. We conducted our tryouts at the conclusion of the 1981 National Championships in Arlington, Texas. We met with most of the players there and invited the ones we wanted to try out in San Diego.

There was so much ability on the floor, we had a difficult time keeping the number of players we brought in to a minimum. In the Dayton years, we'd never had this luxury.

However, we didn't have much time to put together a team before our first domestic tour with Brazil. That tour, through California, was a nine-match affair that provided us with our first taste of pressure unrelated to an opponent.

We were playing in California, our home state, and many of the players' parents and friends were there. These kids were trying to impress all those folks, and we played tight. The team never did relax.

It's ironic that we started our training against Brazil, because we would meet them in the final at the Olympics. Brazil was a good team, one that had finished fifth in the Moscow Olympics of 1980.

The first match was at the University of California at San Diego and was held in a sold-out 2,500-seat gym. Sunderland, Duwelius, and Berzins were with us. So were Tim Hovland, Sinjin Smith, Mike Dodd, and Randy Stoklos. We lost that first match, although we played well. We still lacked training and we didn't have much of a team defensive concept. Yet it was an auspicious beginning. We ended up winning five of the nine matches, but could never pull away from that team, or them from us. In fact, all of our competitions with Brazil, even through the Olympics, were close.

During that tour we began to have real problems with Smith and Hovland. We lost Stoklos, who decided the structured program was not for him. However, we gained Kiraly, who had finally finished the school term. He was our most significant addition.

Kiraly we knew was a magnificent player, which led to our handling him differently than the others. All our players are individuals and we have to make sure we deal with each on his own level, but Kiraly stands alone as a volleyball player.

That's why we drove him so hard. If we had a practice and Kiraly performed as well as, say, Saunders, there was something wrong. Kiraly should be better than Saunders. We were always more demanding of him because of what he could do, and it helped that he had the same attitude about himself. He expected to do better than the others. When he didn't, he was unhappy.

He was more than a volleyball player. He was an athlete. Several months after the Olympics, Kiraly participated in one of those Superstar contests and tied, with Mark Gastineau of the New York Jets, for first place.

With Kiraly, we felt set for our next competition, the Zone Championships, a qualifier for the World Championships. The Zones were held in Mexico City in July. We had some of the best training we'd ever had for those Zones and took advantage of Hovland, Kiraly, and Dvorak's skills. Yet we were still looking for inside blockers. We had people capable of blocking in the middle, but nobody who could play there with consistent effectiveness.

At our arrival in Mexico City, we were greeted with bad news. Mike Dodd, a starter who had previously played professionally, was declared ineligible. He hadn't received proper clearance to become an amateur again. He stayed with us the rest of the year, but eventually left to play club volleyball in Italy until his situation could be resolved.

Without Dodd, we learned more about the other players. We also learned about an unfortunate team trait that would become a problem that would continue even into the Olympics. The team's perception of an opponent's ability often influenced our level of play against that opponent.

When there seemed to be little reason to be highly motivated, the team wasn't. We sometimes took certain opponents too lightly. Our seemingly insurmountable leads were often frittered away. It made no difference. We were better, and knowing that made us feel superior. Just knowing we should have beaten a team appeared to be enough.

Even with that kind of thinking, we breezed through our round-robin competition, beating Guatemala, the Dominican Republic, Panama, and Mexico. We looked forward to playing Cuba in the finals.

First, we had to play Canada in the semis, and that was a tough, five-game match. Blanchard came off the bench to turn it around. Berzins was also magnificent in that Canadian match, and from then on, we didn't have any problems with Canada, a team we played many times. But the closeness of the match was solely the result of not taking them seriously until it was almost too late.

Canada eventually became a very fine team, able to beat a number of good teams, but they never beat us in any important tournament.

Our final match with Cuba was in the very arena where the 1968 Olympic Games had been played. I remember warming up that night and how confident my team and staff were.

There was only one warmup gym for the two teams, the same as there would be in the Olympics. In that situation, mind games usually go on, the teams try to show off to gain an advantage. Then, one of the two nets in use broke, and the teams had to warm up on the same court. There were some real heavy intimidation tactics going on, but I thought we held our own.

Usually, I was the one who expressed apprehension and Neville was the eternal optimist. We'd play at predicting games on every match — a ritual before each game. We rarely agreed, except for the gold medal match!

No matter how much we prepared for a match, I could think of things we'd forgotten. I could see problems, not so much with the players, but with the match plan. I was never satisfied. Neville and I laughed about it, especially going into the gold medal match.

Before the Cuban match, I had a rare moment of giddy confidence. Yes, we would win. We led, 13-12, in the fifth game, but could not win. I was disappointed, but knew we were just as good.

In that match we saw something special in Timmons, and knew down the road he could be a great player for us. But we lost. Cuba scored its last two points on our consecutive hitting errors.

In spite of it all, Neville was upbeat about how we performed. We were mainly concerned about how we made errors under pressure, but we realized our tactics were working.

As badly as I felt about losing, I was more displeased with what happened afterward. There are very stylized rules and a lot of protocol in international volleyball. After we lost this emotional match, Hovland and Kiraly fell flat on their backs on the floor as if they had just lost everything — their closest relative, the gold medal, or their first born.

It was an attempt to show they had given their all and failed, yet it came off as rude, immature behavior. It also sent a distasteful message to the others on the team: "We played 110 percent and you other dogs let us down." That's disruptive to the team and insensitive behavior. We had to knock that out of our players as best we could.

In our team meetings, the players used to talk about what winners they were. But an athlete has to know how to lose to become a winner. All he can do is the best he can, and if he loses, he loses.

That tournament also brought another problem to light. When Kiraly was left off the tournament all-star team in favor of Duwelius, Blanchard, Dvorak, and Hovland, there was a lot of bitter joking about the selections. The chosen players were not complimented as they should have been. It let us in on the idea that this team might never be close-knit.

The rest of the summer I talked to our players about being good teammates. A rift was developing, which we would have to face, and at times the situation was uncomfortable.

And a bad process was developing. Players would come in coachable, then decide they knew it all and question every move. That kind of thinking had to be broken down, and was, but in the meantime, it was difficult to handle.

I had to counsel Sunderland and Waldie the first two years in Dayton. They didn't want to do the things I wanted done because they were so good and they knew it. But a coach can't have two kinds of training exercises, one for the top players, one for the rest. It can devastate a team when the star players make it obvious they're better than the others. We're all one team and all have to play together. Eventually, Sunderland and Waldie understood that, especially after we acquired players better than they were. It's a tough lesson to learn and not all our athletes learned it.

Some of the problem can be traced to an interview I gave about what I perceived as "The California Attitude." Being an athlete traditionalist, I couldn't understand some attitudes I observed on the west coast. I said many of those who played in California and particularly on the beach were prima donnas. What I meant was that the psychology of the beach creates prima donnas.

Well, I guess that means the same thing. But the beach and the players attached to it were not my ideal, and they didn't care for my comments, either.

The beach is generally a playground. Beach play certainly is serious and competitive on the pro circuit, but it also causes problems in a program like ours. Only two players are on a team, and players only have to relate to one partner. On a regular team, six players have to be aware of each other.

Also, on the beach, officiating is loose and players are used to complaining and screaming about it. Calls are hardly ever questioned in the more structured indoor game.

Worst of all, beach volleyball's environment lends itself to all kinds of excesses that seem to go hand in hand with sports, like liquor and drugs. There's a body adulation, a body culture, a "holier than thou" attitude, and the play can be more recreational than competitive.

There are also technical differences. The blocking techniques and some of the rules are different. A player is not allowed over the net in beach volleyball, but of course blocking over the net is a must indoors. Passing and setting differ, too.

Certainly, there is some carryover between the sports. The best tennis players have probably played squash or racquetball at one time or another. However, it is unlikely John McEnroe or Jimmy Connors still plays those sports, and they never play them to train for tennis.

I felt that players growing up in the beach environment could cause problems. Calling them prima donnas was being kind in many cases, but less than diplomatic, and it certainly caused some rifts on our team over the years. We had several graduates of beach volleyball, and most of those players couldn't understand why I didn't like it.

Still, I allowed some participation in our first year, then cut off beach volleyball altogether. After repeated abuse of my rules on the subject, the beach game was verboten.

Our next competition was our first annual tour to Japan in late July and early August. We played five matches and lost them all. Volleyball is popular there and all the matches were televised. That gave our players the feeling they were doing something significant and that somewhere in the world people really cared about the sport.

Four of the five matches went to five games, and in one, we led 14-4 in the fifth game. The motivation problem resurfaced. We began playing the situation instead of playing each point. We were so far ahead, we didn't think we could lose, whereas the Japanese played at the top of their abilities, one point at a time.

We tried to get our players to ignore the score. Each point was its own game. Sure, it looked easy at 14-4, only one point to go. But there is no time element in volleyball, no exact number of innings to play.

All the Japanese had to do was keep scoring, and they did.

During that tour, I had more run-ins with Hovland. We had only one rule on the team, although it may have seemed like we had 1,000 rules. Never disgrace our team or our country. That was it. Everything else stemmed from that simple philosophy.

In my estimation, the way we acted at certain competitions was a disgrace.

We returned to the United States with the Japanese team and took three out of four matches, which indicates what a home-country advantage can do. By the end of the tour, we felt dominant over Japan, and we hadn't even won the two-country series. To us, it was how we ended up that counted, not how we began.

On the first night back, we beat them in a five-game match in San Diego. It was the first time a U.S. team had beaten Japan since 1969.

We trained mostly with small tours and exhibitions spiced with tournaments. They served a dual purpose. They gave us live competition to practice against, and helped raise necessary funds.

Brazil came up and played two matches, winning the first in five games at Pepperdine near Los Angeles, then losing to us at UC San Diego.

Our first important tournament after that was the Canada Cup, played in frigid Winnipeg. Trust me, nobody took beach clothes along. These matches were important for us, even though we weren't at full strength, because Cuba was there and it would give us a chance to measure our progress.

Our roster was cut a bit. Kiraly and Timmons were back in school and Dodd had left, but we won our opening match against Canada, 3-0.

Then we lost to Cuba in five. We were still playing around with our starting lineup and trying to make a decision on Powers. We started him against Cuba and he was as bad as I'd ever seen him. Powers was cut at the end of the competition, but we knew he'd be back. He just needed some more seasoning, mostly emotionally.

We thought with a few personnel changes we'd be able to handle Cuba easily, which is strange to say since Cuba had always dominated us. But there were indications that our training was paying off.

The next night, we beat Brazil, 3-0, one of the few 3-0 matches we would have with that team. Cuba also won its semi, against Brazil, while we beat Canada again in ours. Then, on November 12, 1981, we did it.

It was the United States vs. Cuba, and they were smug. After three close games, we led 2-1. Then we made some subs that changed not only the tempo of the match, but our outlook on who should be playing for us more regularly.

Berzins and Smith went in, giving us a small lineup, but one that won easily in four games. The small lineup seemed to be a workable alternative to the usual big-guys-only look. Part of developing a team is finding out who can play, where, and which combinations work best.

Hovland was named the tournament's MVP, It was the last match he would play for the United States.

We certainly finished 1981, our first complete year in San Diego, on a high note. We won the gold medal in the Canada Cup, our first international tournament victory of any kind, and set the stage for our quadrennial.

There was trouble ahead, even in this San Diego paradise. It was almost ruinous, but somehow we held together and worked out our problems. The next year would be rough. Very rough.

Chapter 7.

Trouble in Paradise.

Training, and our matches, were going too smoothly. The team that needed motivation to stay at its best seemed to thrive on controversy also.

The most severe blow to our tranquility revolved around Tim Hovland. He and Sinjin Smith eventually filed grievances with the USVBA long after they left the team.

In addition, some players and their parents tried to have me removed as coach.

It was serious stuff, situations that had to be dealt with carefully. None of the problems that occurred in the eight years since our program began consumed as much time as these incidents.

Hovland was not cut. I'd prefer to say he quit the team, which in my recollection of events, is how it actually happened.

I had been accused of being prejudiced against both Smith and Hovland, and they documented that I told them I did not like them. It was a moot point. My personal feelings had nothing to do with their not staying on the team. They just would not work within our system and allow us to have a smooth-running operation, so they had to go.

They were both exceptional players and athletes, though. Hovland was especially good. Yet, as I've said many times, there are other qualities and abilities needed to build a team. Just being a good player isn't enough.

Certainly we put up with some deviant behavior among players good enough to play. However, they all eventually worked within our system. It was the feeling of many of those connected with our program that Smith and Hovland were not making the necessary adjustments.

Smith especially was always unhappy about something and was convinced I didn't like him. He was right, but I don't remember saying so in those exact words. He also felt the program was failing him because he couldn't find a job.

As an amateur sports operation, we really overextended ourselves when we first moved to San Diego. We made some promises that we couldn't keep out of a genuine desire to provide the most complete training center possible. We also wanted jobs for the players to be better than the ones in Dayton. And we wanted those jobs to be available immediately.

Initially, we went to great expense to be first class, which later led to money problems, which further led to complaints by some players, especially Smith and Hovland.

We paid player travel expenses to San Diego for their interviews with the coaches and program principals. Then we paid for moving expenses. These were unheard-of benefits at that time and they nearly exhausted our financial resources. When we didn't get them jobs as soon as expected, we tried to subsidize our players with money. It quickly ran out.

This was folly.

Some of our players did begin their San Diego careers sleeping on apartment floors. Things were tough for them and they had to put up with a lot for the privilege of working hard for rewards they wouldn't receive until later. But what constitutes hardship depends on your point of view. The players who had spent a lot of time in Dayton didn't complain at all about San Diego.

We couldn't deliver on all of our promises right away and tried to be honest with our players. If they couldn't afford to be on the team, they could leave. That isn't the way we wanted it, but we had growing pains and did our best. Every time a player came in and said he absolutely had to have money, he got it. They thought it was from a special volleyball reserve fund. It was usually out of my pocket.

It had to be this way. I wanted the program to survive, and did what I could to make it succeed. Some percentage of any team's success is financially based, whether we like to admit it or not, and certain players have to be helped more than others. At NCAA schools, additional financial help violates rules. In our situation, additional help was bankrupting us.

Smith was in Dayton for awhile in 1979 and 1980 when we trained for the Pan American Games and final 1980 Olympic qualifier. He's a talented athlete, as talented an athlete as I've coached. He became a full-time team member in 1981 because I wanted him.

When he tried out for the team in 1981, we had a number of volleyball coaches helping to make the selections. Nobody else wanted Smith on the team, and that means nobody. Everybody said he'd be trouble. He didn't have a real position. He was part setter and part hitter.

Well, that's when I made the mistake. I alone wanted him. He was a great athlete. I figured I could find a spot for him. But everybody was right. He gave me nothing but trouble.

Smith's problem had to do with money, although he was a disruptive influence on the team regardless of his financial status.

We told team members we would try to find them jobs where they could work part time, practice and travel part time and still make about $1,000 a month. If we couldn't find jobs immediately, we tried to subsidize the players until the jobs were forthcoming.

It didn't take long for the money to run out. Our jobs program, headed by Klostermann, was a good one, but in one sense we were handicapped by our closeness to Los Angeles. Since many of the players grew up there, they would visit on their off days instead of interviewing for jobs.

Smith was the complete California beach boy. A fashion model — he makes a good living doing that today — he was always concerned with the way he looked. Naturally, his was the California look, which isn't always appropriate, especially in the business environment.

In our jobs program, some of the initiative has to be put on the player. We can set up the interviews and provide leads, but the player has to follow through. Smith did not make a good presentation at interviews and he did not follow through.

We tried harder than he did to find him a job.

The real split came with an apparent misunderstanding of how we would operate during a two-month "break" early in 1982. There shouldn't have been any misunderstanding at all.

During that period, a training time between competitions, Smith secured a modeling job in New York. He asked permission to work there, and I said he could go for two weeks. The rest of the squad was staying in San Diego on self-motivated workout programs. We also had some public relations chores to attend to.

Later, when Smith learned that the work in New York required travel, he requested a two-week extension. I granted him the additional leave. Another mistake.

That was in January and we had matches scheduled at the beginning of March. How any player could have thought we were taking two months off from any training is beyond me, but that's the way Smith interpreted the schedule. He had a real conflict between modeling and volleyball, and he couldn't understand why being in San Diego prior to those matches was so important.

He stayed in New York the entire two months and had his mother contact me as to his whereabouts. Finally, when he didn't show, we figured he was gone for good and had chosen modeling over the volleyball team. We wrapped up practice and left for our matches in Bellingham, Washington and other northwest cities.

One morning at 5:30, Smith called from New York — he had a difficult time figuring out the time difference. He wanted to know how things were going and was just keeping in touch. I said, "Great, now that you're no longer with the team."

He filed a grievance with the USVBA a year later, saying he really wanted to be a team member but was kicked off the team because I didn't like him.

He had had one great match for us at the Canada Cup when we beat Cuba for the first time. Other than that, his performance was erratic. He was late to practices and only wanted to play with his friend and beach partner Kiraly.

Smith listed several charges in his grievance, all of which I answered candidly in a letter to the USVBA that was my statement in the case. I considered his claims erroneous, many ridiculous. Except his claim that I didn't like him. I didn't. But if a player lived by our rules and was good enough to play, he stayed on our team, regardless of my personal opinion.

The USVBA heard Smith's case and backed me up; the paper work on the matter lasted well into 1984.

The USVBA also backed me through an attempted plot to remove me from my job, a situation potentially more damaging than that involving Smith.

In the summer of 1981, before Smith became an issue, some parents became impatient and fabricated program problems. They created huge issues out of our temporary growing pains, yet never called me or anyone directly associated with the team to hear our side. They only heard from a few disgruntled players. They began writing letters to the president of the USVBA, Bob Lindsay, an oil man from Texas. Bob was very supportive of our training center and of me personally. Unfortunately he was not aware of all of the particulars of the San Diego program, and so he couldn't respond specifically to the parents' charges.

One of the parents, Laz Kiraly, even went to Al Scates, the popular UCLA coach, asked Scates if he'd like the job, and tried to involve him in the whole affair. They thought they could go behind my back, pressure the USVBA to remove me, and set up a program in their own image. They had every position filled in this dream world training center, and they even had the center positioned in their own backyard. The lure of the job caused Scates to listen. He didn't offer to take the job, but his willingness to listen didn't help me much at that point.

When I found out what was happening, the USVBA insisted they could handle it and that I should not confront the parents. When we lost that five-game match to Cuba in the Zones, we qualified for the World Championships, but not the World Cup. This was used as evidence that I was incompetent. We hadn't even been practicing together a full month.

When I found out how persistent the parents had become, and when our schedule allowed for it, I insisted on meeting with their principal spokesperson. In late 1981, I met with Laz Kiraly and Ron Salmons, another parent, on my own. I told the USVBA of my plans and they reluctantly agreed. I guess they were afraid I was going to make matters worse, but I promised to hold my temper and try to reason out our differences.

We had lunch in San Diego, and we should have done it earlier. They presented their problems and grievances, and I presented my point of view and rationale.

By that time, we had won the Canada Cup and finished the year in good shape. I think they already knew they weren't going to remove me from my position, and we had a very frank discussion.

What came out of it is that they became strong supporters, first for the team, then for the program, and finally for me. Both apologized, and while I still don't think they liked or agreed with me and my philosophy, they at least understood what we were trying to accomplish. Laz Kiraly is an especially outspoken, strong, and domineering person. In spite of his initial antagonism, he's been very good for the team and an active and contributing supporter.

The attempt to remove me died a silent death. It never gained much momentum, and not much was known or written about it. The volleyball team just carried on as if nothing were happening, and we began to win. You don't get as many complaints when you win.

The Hovland case was much more volatile. I stayed with this guy longer than I should have because he is arguably the best player in the country.

A team's coach learns quickly that players differ from one another. Treating them in the same manner is a mistake. We tried to slow Hovland down. He lived in the fast lane and was determined to operate by a separate set of rules.

He is so talented though, I felt under some pressure to keep him. I made special concessions that were controversial to say the least. None of it worked. I was burned for some of my decisions, but I still recognize his talent. He was voted MVP at the National Championships one year, and I was one of the guys who voted for him — a year after he quit the team.

On the court, he usually delivered on his promises and he wasn't much trouble at practice or during games. Unreliability was his problem — he was often late or absent. He had more car problems than Chuck Muncie of the San Diego Chargers, and he commonly showed up for practices in less than perfect condition.

After the Canada Cup in 1981, he wanted to go back to USC to finish school, which was fine with us and part of our philosophy. He also had a job with a bank in San Diego. He told us not to worry about the job; he would have it transferred to Los Angeles while he was in school, which he did. He didn't tell the bank, however, that he also had a scholarship and didn't intend to show up much at work.

When the bank called us about this problem, we covered up for Hovland as best we could and tried to warn him of what was happening. Eventually, he was terminated, but the bank told him that when he finished school and moved back to San Diego they might rehire him. Later, Hovland used this to demonstrate how we were against him.

Then, at the 1982 Nationals in Hilo, Hawaii, when we were not in training and allowed our players to participate with other club teams, Hovland got into an embarrassing yelling match with Duwelius, who was playing for another team.

It was a completely inappropriate display of bad language and behavior. Hovland and Rich were teammates and the Nationals were supposed to be a relaxing break from the rigors of National Team training. It demonstrated his complete lack of respect for and interest in his teammates and the program.

In spite of all that, we wanted him back. Hovland, though, wanted everything. He wanted his job, he wanted to play, to play on the beach, to play in Italy where he could make some money.

When the time came to report for the team, he missed appointments, he missed practices, he came up with excuses. His father was ill. His car wouldn't start. He still hadn't shown three or four days after that, and I called him. I still wanted him on the team. I told him if he didn't show up, we would know he had chosen to withdraw from the team.

He was also told that we would not pay his car fare from Los Angeles to San Diego and that he would have to apologize to the rest of the team for being late. No way was he going to do that.

He played the rest of the summer on the beach.

In the fall, Hovland went to Italy and made a large sum of money. When he returned late in December, we got together and, crazily, I told him he could return. Tim Hovland is a great player and I felt we needed him since we hadn't done well at the World Championships. I also thought he wanted to get back on the team badly. What he wanted was to get back on his own terms. I'm sure he felt we would come to him and accept him under all and any conditions, but our program came first.

I tried to talk him into going on our Outward Bound trip. If he had agreed to that, I think everyone associated with the team would have welcomed him back gladly. He said he had some matters to take care of in Italy and couldn't go. I even allowed him to get away with that. I told him to be in San Diego in mid-February. I didn't hear from him until mid-May.

The sun must have been getting to me. I still wanted him back. I tried to find ways to get him to rejoin the team. Even parents of the other players were calling for him to be reinstated. No one had confidence in our ability to perform without him.

That's when I came up with our "bonding" proposal in the late spring of 1983. Something everyone could live with. He would pay the USVBA a sum of money — about $1,000 a month, all at once — and we would hold it for him to be repaid monthly against his good behavior. He thought about it, then agreed.

He still hadn't practiced with us, so we went to our Zone Championships in Indianapolis without him. He was supposed to meet me, after the Zones to make certain everything was set; he never showed. Instead, he told the media I wanted him to buy his way back on the team. That the "bonding" idea didn't work out might have been predictable. That we wanted it to work was undeniable. That the details of our tried-for arrangement, some of them wrong, were aired in the media was reprehensible. I credit some of that to Hovland, the rest to the media.

We were not asking him to buy his way back on the team. That was absolutely wrong. We wanted to buy some assurances he wouldn't cause any more problems for us. The idea of a refundable fine seemed workable. Our plan might have been controversial and unprecedented, but it was legitimate and well conceived.

He had missed more than one year of the program. He had made lots of money in the sport. The rest of the players had stuck with the program and sacrificed those years and believed in the team. The players had to know Hovland was making sacrifices, too, or else we might have had other defections.

The deal also detracted from our accomplishments. We were winning the Zones, but all anybody wanted to talk about was our "bonding" agreement with Hovland. I denied the whole thing, but responded carefully to the questions to avoid any out-and-out lies. We sure were getting a lot of publicity, though.

There were a couple of reasons we didn't want to present our whole side of the story. First, we didn't want to get into a public debate over the issue. Second, we thought it would be impossible to get a complete airing in the media of such a complex issue.

It was probably a mistake to be dealing with Hovland anyway. I was never certain we were doing the right thing. He never met me after the Zones, and that was it. After spending so much time and energy trying to get Hovland back on the team, we let the matter drop, although his grievance was still pending.

The situation split the team and later, at our August Pre-Olympics Quest for Gold tournament in Long Beach, Hovland showed up, conspicuously, to watch us. His appearance and the surrounding controversy unnerved our team. Some of the guys were still his friends and to have him around and not playing was tough to take. Other guys tried too hard just to prove he wasn't needed. We lost to Japan, our only loss at home in all of 1983.

It would be unfair to blame that loss on Hovland, because our team was pretty tired by that time, but Hovland was a disruptive influence. Amazingly, when he showed up at the tournament, his brother, a lawyer, handed McPeak a signed letter agreeing to all our terms — including the "bonding" agreement — so he could return to the team. The letter was rejected. We were through trying to deal with Tim Hovland.

At the end of that year Hovland's grievance was rejected, and he went back to Italy to play another season of volleyball there.

I don't know if he was in the arena when we won the gold medal or not. I certainly hope he was.

Needless to say, my relationship with the media was not always sterling. In fact, I hated interviews and repeatedly answering the same questions. For most of our time in San Diego, I wanted Neville to handle the media. He liked doing it and was good at it. I gave interviews only when a story was being done specifically about me or when some reporter refused to talk to anybody else.

That worked fine until we got to Los Angeles. The reporters there insisted on talking only to head coaches, so all Neville could do was set up interviews. I had to do the talking.

I pride myself on being honest and candid, but being too candid can get a person into trouble.

Actually, I enjoy talking to members of the media outside of interview situations. I was having a good time the night I told four or five reporters at the Games that much of the media was "stupid, petty, and ill-informed." I wasn't talking about the people sitting in front of me. I was just making some generalizations about the way we had been covered, and venting my frustrations over our lack of exposure and publicity.

When my quote appeared in all the newspapers the next day, and later in the magazines, I thought it was blown out of proportion. I saw no reason to backtrack on my feelings just because it looked bad in print, though. For the most part, I think my perceptions were pretty accurate. Besides, we felt that if there had to be any controversy at the Olympics, it should center around the coaches and not the players. They already had enough pressure on them, and didn't need a lot of reporters bugging them about being the favorites, and so on. They were trying to meet the expectations of a lot of people, many of whom they didn't even know. It was better to have the major focus on me.

My media problem was largely the result of the lack of attention we received during the previous four years. We got virtually no publicity at all until we went to the Soviet Union in early May. We won four matches and were suddenly discovered. Newspapers and major magazines wanted a piece of us, not because we won, but because the Soviet boycott was declared.

The reaction implied that all the good teams were suddenly out of the tournament, and we would win by default. Over the next three or four months, people jumped on the bandwagon of the men's team as the gold medal favorite. They were people who had never written a word about volleyball and weren't even interested in it.

All of a sudden the Olympics were at hand, and I was supposed to provide a history of the previous four years for a media that hadn't paid much attention. We were being picked as favorites, but for the wrong reasons. It should have been because we were good and not because some of the other teams weren't going to participate. And if we were favorites, where were all the stories about our accomplishments?

It caused me a great deal of frustration. I was torn between accommodating the media because the sport needs all the attention it can get, and chewing them out every chance I got because of their lack of attention during the four years prior to the Games. Amateur sports has been neglected by the members of the media, who have some catching up to do.

My biggest problem was with a sportswriter for the *Los Angeles Times* who had been assigned to volleyball at the Olympics. Essentially, at issue was the way he handled the Hovland case. I thought a couple of things this reporter did were extremely unethical.

And these unethical dealings continued with our team and with the women's team and the women's coach, right up through the Olympic Games — in fact, even after the games.

The first time I met this reporter, we were in San Diego. He came for lunch and we spent a great deal of time together. He was ostensibly writing an article about me and the program.

As it turns out, although the article was largely about me, he was a bit inaccurate concerning Hovland and gave the wrong impression of my position. We were still undecided about how we would deal with Tim, but the article implied that we had decided to invite him back. I did not say that. Hovland did. Later, the reporter acknowledged his confusion. But the damage was done, to our integrity and the team's morale.

Everybody makes mistakes, but when they appear in print, the effect can be magnified.

I admit I have a bias. The sports media is always looking for a story, under the guise of looking for news. By definition, the news is something people want to read about. The people writing often don't have any more expertise than the average Joe on the street. I don't think they always exercise their power judiciously and I feel there is tremendous editorializing at the expense of accuracy. The kind of reporting that appears on sports pages would not be tolerated on the front page.

Not many people at major news outlets were interested in us, but this guy at the *Times* was. He telephoned me many times, primarily while I was in Indianapolis, after he found out about the Hovland situation, and tried to make me admit to an arrangement with Hovland to have him return to the team.

We certainly didn't want our arrangement with Hovland to be publicized since there were so many ways it could be misinterpreted. We especially didn't want it handled by a medium that didn't always wield its power judiciously. It was a delicate situation, and we wanted it to be handled in a delicate manner. The potential for misunderstanding was enormous.

Worse than that was a situation just before we went to Indianapolis. The same reporter arrived as we were completing practice. He talked to me at the end of our session for about a half hour, took no notes, and had no tape recorder. It was my impression the two of us were just discussing the team. I gave him a lot of background, much of which I didn't expect or want to see in print.

I was frank about a number of topics I never would have discussed had I known they would be "on the record." He ran the entire interview. I don't even know how he remembered it all, unless he was wired. I felt he clearly violated the normal interview relationship by not informing me the subjects we discussed were for the record.

After that, I did my best to avoid him. He was more interested in digging into the controversy surrounding the team than in reporting how the team performed.

Certainly, controversy is the media's interest, too. But we had come so far in the actual playing area, I thought we might get some good coverage out of that. Even with all the controversy surrounding the Los Angeles Raiders football team, most articles eventually got around to talking about what a good club it was.

There was also a problem with the media at the Games. Several reporters talked with me about the most elementary aspects of our team. They asked things I felt should have been obvious or known by that point, particularly by people picking us to win the gold medal. They didn't know how we qualified, or where. They didn't know our match record leading into the Games, or who our best players were.

I guess I lost my composure and temper a number of times.

The USVBA and other officials thought one of my responsibilities was to educate the media. I certainly didn't think so. My responsiblity was to coach the team, and I think I did a damn good job.

If members of the media want to think of me as a loud-mouthed jerk, so be it. A lot of other successful people in our society have lived through that, and so will I.

Chapter 8.

Corporate sponsorship.
And don't forget Tom Selleck.

I was airbrushed right out of the Ford Bronco advertisement. Even with my handsome face, they zapped me. Said I didn't smile enough. I told them *I was smiling.*

What they did to me was worse than what they do to the *Playboy Magazine* models. They didn't just airbrush out the bumps and bruises, they airbrushed everything.

Through the efforts of McPeak, we gradually garnered a large network of corporate sponsorships, which meant money for us and good publicity for them. One of our sponsors was Ford, which had us endorse the Bronco II.

A bunch of us — Neville, Sunderland, Duwelius, Wilde, Timmons, Salmons, Marlowe, and I — went out to Dog Beach in San Diego to do the filming.

I was driving a Bronco near the water and the guys were running alongside or hanging out the windows throwing volleyballs around. The director was also running alongside with his cameraman, screaming at me to drive more in the water. Drive more in the water? I was afraid I was going to lose the thing!

I was also told to smile more. The guy just couldn't understand that I *was* smiling. But it wasn't enough.

After the pictures were developed, one was chosen, and I was removed. Oh, well.

During our Dayton years, we had a couple of sponsors who supplied us with uniforms — Jelenk, a sporting goods company, followed by Descente, a Japanese clothing company, who provided our uniforms for competition. They didn't make shoes, so we used Adidas.

Years earlier, Adidas tried to get into the uniform act, with lackluster results. They sent us a bunch of sweatsuits with the USA Olympic logo. They must have thought we were all the size of Wilt Chamberlain because most of the uniforms would have fit him with room to spare. We gave them out to the guys at Christmas, told them to wash them in hot water and dry fully, then use them as sleepwear on cold nights.

The guys never turned down free clothing. It wouldn't matter if I had just handed out 12 pair of socks to each guy. They always wanted more, maybe for relatives and friends; they didn't even bother to make up elaborate excuses. Sometimes I thought they wanted the uniforms more than a spot in the starting lineup.

The most natural sponsor for any athletic team is a uniform company. When we got to San Diego, Mizuno offered the best deal for our uniforms. Mizuno made quality equipment for us, which everyone liked real well.

At least we had plenty of uniforms. When I played, the team manager would go to a sporting goods company and pick up uniforms off the rack, usually two shirts and shorts to a player. There was a lot of washing in hotel sinks on those early tours.

McPeak became our contact for our other big sponsors almost by mistake. He was with the USVBA for some time when they had a meeting on future planning. Nobody wanted to go out and ask for money. They all wanted to hire professional fund raisers instead. McPeak said he'd take over this area so we wouldn't have to pay for it.

He did a great job, and learned a lot about the business of sponsors and contract support. He searched for money full time, and was a savior for us financially.

For instance, in 1981, Coors Beer was signed to sponsor our domestic tours. The contract was delayed because the history of the USVBA is YMCA-based, and many of those members couldn't fathom getting involved with a beer company. Finally, they relented, and Coors became a sponsor.

Unfortunately, we allowed the beer company to use the wording "The Coors USA Volleyball Team." That was a mistake we didn't repeat once we became more sophisticated. We weren't the Coors team, we were the USA team.

Coors also sponsored the National Championships and the Junior National Championships. To help advertise the games, we wore Coors Beer patches on our uniform sleeves.

The next year, when Coors dropped out, Anheuser Busch and Michelob Light sponsored our domestic tours. They gave us more support money and stayed with us through the Olympics. We also wore a patch for them, and they sent us a lot of free beer. The guys loved our contracts with beer companies. It defrayed party expenses. Seriously, they were great supporters — in major promotions and in little ways with local distributor events.

We had other sponsors, too. Union Carbide named its Eveready Super Heavy Duty battery as the official battery of the U.S. Men's and Women's

Volleyball Teams. There wasn't much up-front money involved with that, but Eveready sponsored some exhibition matches on the east coast. They did a huge national promotion for us tied into Tom Selleck posters.

The most patches we wore at one time was two, one on each sleeve, so we didn't look too much like human billboards. But sometimes it was tough to remember who was sponsoring what.

We also had an agreement with the Syntex drug company for an inflammation-reducing drug that they donated to us. They advertised in trade journals. Atari, Jell-o, and Viviane Woodard cosmetics did some work for the women's team. Miller's Outpost, a clothing company, helped sponsor youth programs and we also did a commercial for them.

Since the Olympics, we have signed a contract with Parker Brothers and its new Nerf volleyball.

Our biggest coup might have been obtaining Tom Selleck as our honorary team captain. We needed a name to help promote our sport, and Selleck, an avid player and a popular actor, was a natural. Tony Crabb knew Selleck because they had played together on a team in Hawaii, a masters club (over age 35) that participated in USVBA national tournaments. Selleck had a natural feeling for the game. He also had played some volleyball in college at Southern Cal.

Crabb called, and Selleck was very much interested.

I can't say enough about Selleck. Some guys lend their names to things and leave it at that. This guy really enjoyed his position with us and considered it an honor.

You'd think the guys on the team would be excited when Selleck came into our locker room before the final match against Brazil, but the look on Selleck's face was also one of appreciation. He was really honored. When we had a victory party after the last match in Los Angeles, he stayed for virtually the entire affair. He even brought his parents. He was a lot more than just a name for us.

Selleck helped in so many ways. In spite of his gruesome shooting schedule, he participated in several fund-raisers. We even managed to put out two posters of Tom in volleyball poses for which he charged no fee. Fuji film shot the posters for free, so we earned virtually 100 percent of the proceeds. We must have sold a half million posters. Maybe it was the USA uniform he was wearing.

The fund-raisers were usually matches, his masters team against another masters team. He knows what he is doing out on the court. And he packed the fans in every place he played.

"Real People" filmed one of our matches and then made a $10,000 donation to the team to boot. Selleck stayed after the matches and signed autographs. His son came to a number of our events in the summer of 1983, and we used him as a ballboy and got him involved in helping out.

The topper came when he was asked to introduce President and Mrs. Reagan at one of the '85 inaugural functions. Selleck told the President that being there was almost as much of a thrill as being at the summer Olympics and watching the Men's Volleyball Team win the gold medal.

With the success we were having with Selleck, the USVBA thought it would be good to have a national spokesperson for all of volleyball, and singer-actor John Davidson signed on. He, too, is a really nice guy and he did some fund-raisers and public service announcements.

The women's team eventually secured an honorary captain, Susan Anton, who didn't make Selleck look so good to us anymore. Sorry, Tom.

We had other local sponsors in San Diego, including the Souplantation, a great soup and salad bar restaurant in the city. They donated five meals a week for each player and staff member and even had special napkins printed up with their logo as the official team training table.

Ponderosa had catered a lot of our meals in Dayton, but usually only when we were on tour with a visiting team. Souplantation did it for us all the time.

We also used the San Diego Sports Medicine Center for training, and companies that provided jobs for our players advertised in our programs.

Our corporate sponsorships were important, and Cliff McPeak can't be thanked enough for his effort. He took our association to the forefront of amateur sports in this important area.

I think that's significant because that's the way amateur sport is going. The U.S. Olympic Committee is increasing its involvement with national sponsors and is encouraging each individual sport to raise additional money on other levels.

Now the companies are more willing to become involved, and in the year leading up to the Olympics, they were throwing themselves at anything that smacked of the Games.

If a company didn't have the money to sponsor something nationally, it went for a specific team, or athlete. Anything. The Games were being played in the United States, and corporations wanted to be a part of them.

This is the American way. When the Soviets pulled out of the Olympics, one of the reasons they gave was the commercialization of the Games. That was a cop out. Their system is run by the government. Ours isn't. In America, we buy and sell. It's the capitalist way. If we could commercialize the Olympics to the point of making them more viable for us, that was great.

Amateur athletics gives a lot in return to companies in the way of recreational value and wholesomeness. We have to take advantage of our salable characteristics, and companies have to realize what we have to offer.

We were one of the first groups to take advantage of this new thinking on selling amateur sports. It has allowed us to make more trips to compete with other teams around the world. There were a few of these trips before, but when they got too expensive, they were often cut. Professional sports had become big time in this country (See, the capitalist way!), and amateur athletes unrelated to football or baseball seemed to be noticed only during the Olympics. How did people expect amateurs to survive between Olympics while training and working, too?

Americans have this feeling that the world's greatest athletes are professionals. That's simply not true, at least in the way we define professional and amateur. Other countries simply have athletes. The Soviet Union has a great sports program because they simply have athletes, no pros and no amateurs. They treat all their athletes the same. Some of their sports are more popular than others, but their structure emphasizes all sports equally.

Sports abroad is extremely political. Athletics are a major government activity, are used to justify the social structure, and are largely government sponsored.

Amateur teams in other countries tend to stay together longer, too. The staffs of the Soviet teams have been intact for 10 years or more. They have the same doctors, the same trainers, the same assistant coaches, and many of the same athletes. For the better athletes in the more popular sports in this country, there are professional outlets. That isn't so for all amateurs, especially ones that don't have professional leagues to join. That's why we are often at a disadvantage in amateur games.

We're playing against the best from other countries with athletes who might not be our best, might not have the training to be the best, or who have to quit or retire before they can become the best.

With more corporate sponsorship, that might change.

Chapter 9.

Who is Doug Beal?

I've sparked a lot of controversy and aired my opinions about volleyball and its players in the last few years, but I think I've got the background to do so.

I first learned the game at Malvern Elementary School in Shaker Heights, Ohio, from Ken Zorge, who was associated with a USVBA club team and was my physical education teacher.

I loved it. I always felt great playing volleyball. I could never get enough of the game. In high school, I'd sit in classes and diagram plays and figure tactics. I don't think I ever threw any volleyball literature away. I was a student of the game from the moment I was introduced to it.

That doesn't mean I was a good player immediately. My first tournament was at the Central YMCA in downtown Cleveland, and I didn't even get to play. That Y had a dumpy gym with a running track around the ceiling. If you got under the track, you couldn't play the ball.

Mark Watson was the club coach at the Y. He believed you could learn and develop as a volleyball player in a handball court, since you could train for hours on ballhandling skills without having to run after the balls. I spent a lot of time on handball courts not only learning, but staying out of the way. The club team was made up of older players, most out of college, and I was just a skinny teenage novice who asked a lot of questions.

Finally, I was taken on a trip, probably because I was so persistent. It wasn't much of a trip, just to the other side of Cleveland.

I never played a minute. They used me to call lines, which was what teams did with their reserve players.

Anyway, I sat in a chair and called the lines for a match that didn't involve our team. I was being nonchalant about it. One of the teams was the St. Joe Lead Company from Meadeville, Pennsylvania. They looked big to me, like coal miners, so I suppose I was happy I wasn't playing. Their uniforms were black and yellow — I remember because they were the ugliest uniforms I have ever seen.

The moment is still very clear to me. I was sitting but should have been standing, and this big bruiser, Bob Mosier (I became friends with him later) hit a ball that smacked my chair so hard I went sprawling. It was a rude awakening for me — one of my dumb moments in volleyball.

Later, I did play for that YMCA club team, and the players on it will always be special to me. They helped give me my start.

In addition to Zorge and Watson, I learned a great deal from Ken Dunlap, my coach at Ohio State. And Carl McGown, Jim Coleman, and later my good friend from Japan, Suguru Furuichi, helped me formulate a strong background in volleyball that would help me synthesize my coaching philosophy.

What I learned from my coaches was voluminous.

Zorge, more than anyone else, established my basic mindset, my overview. He taught me about sports in general. He had a traditional, conservative approach to athletics, and believed in fundamentals and the work ethic. Play as hard as possible for as long as possible. He laid a solid foundation for me and many of his values were woven into our training center.

Watson had a profound affect on me, first when I played and later as I coached. Watson was intensely competitive. He never backed down from a challenge. From him I learned tactics and the creative ways players could be used. He was always developing systems to fit certain players' abilities. He was never inhibited by what had gone before, or the so-called "right way" to do something.

Dunlap, who is out of coaching now, had a background in more traditional American sports — baseball, football, and basketball. He couldn't understand why volleyball wasn't being treated seriously. He taught me how to run a complete program, from equipment purchasing, budgeting, and scheduling, to player conditioning. I used to hang around his office in St. John Arena, milking him for everything he knew.

Originally, I attended Hobart College in Geneva, N.Y., but transferred to Ohio State after we couldn't get a volleyball team established. At OSU, I could continue my career and meet some established volleyball people, such as Jim Coleman.

Coleman introduced me to international volleyball. I learned some sophisticated terminology and concepts when I played for him on the 1970 U.S. team. He opened my eyes to the whole arena of international sport. He taught me dedication. I haven't known anyone as dedicated to his sport as Coleman. He added tremendously to my knowledge of tactics, team play, and prioritizing tasks.

Learning what it was like to play internationally was important. In 1964, at the Tokyo Olympics, the U.S. team didn't even know the internatonal game rules. The United States had been playing to one set of rules and four days before the first match, we found out there was a different set of rules. That's how naive we were.

I guess I shouldn't forget Harlan Cohen, either. He was actually the first coach I played for internationally when I was selected for the 1969 Maccabiah Games in Israel. Cohen had coached the women's national teams in 1966-68 and was the first coach in the country to try the Oriental ideas of training and defense. Before Cohen, they used to roll a few balls out on the court and scrimmage. No one ever thought about practicing hour after hour the way they do in other sports.

Cohen used to talk to me in cliches about percentage volleyball. I used to pass them off, but later in my career, I found myself falling back on what he used to say. Those cliches turned out to be very useful.

"Serve to the same guy you've been serving to," he'd say. "Always play so the sideline is by your outside foot," and "Always set your best hitter until he gets stopped," or "Hit your best shot all the time, don't do anything fancy."

Those kinds of things don't always happen on a volleyball court, but the advice is good. Once the fundamentals are established, a player can experiment.

McGown, who was Coleman's assistant before he became the U.S. head coach, taught me about modern volleyball tactics. I used him as a sounding board to firm up most of my concepts when I began coaching. He was a great defensive thinker.

Furuichi opened me up to other ways of doing things. If a person looks at a chess board from the same side all the time, only the obvious moves appear available. As soon as the board is turned, other moves come to light.

The Russians and Japanese see volleyball differently than we do. Furuichi opened my mind to those points of view.

My background includes many other extensive volleyball influences. I drew ideas from many people in volleyball who have allowed me to more rationally develop my own system. I think the good coaches in all sports do this.

Although I had always considered myself a player, I could never be a great one. I forced myself into the long-range goal of coaching. Three of the men I played under were particularly influential in pointing me toward my coaching goal. First was Watson, then Dunlap, and finally McGown.

I graduated from Ohio State in 1970 and went to Bowling Green to get an M.Ed. I started a varsity volleyball program there, and coached the team from 1970 through December, 1971, when I returned to OSU to work on my Ph.D. in exercise physiology. Dunlap was leaving OSU at that time, so I took over the volleyball team there on a part-time basis.

During the summers, I played on the National Team, and later played for a new club league in southern California that paid minimal support money. I think it was about $500 a month. It was called the Winston League, and had about five or six teams supported by the USVBA and a group of local businessmen in the Los Angeles-San Diego area. The schedule lasted 30-40 games, which helped prepare players for the National Team.

The USVBA hired Furuichi to help train the better players in the league, the ones who would go on to form the basis of our National Team. I became his official host in a way, and we became good friends. We lived together in Orange

County. He knew things about volleyball that had never even crossed my mind.

By 1975, when the league started, I left Ohio State and played more. I felt I was heading into my prime as a player, and wanted to make the most of it. I hated to admit it, but by 1976, I was effectively finished as a player. (That's a short "prime.") I had surgery on my shoulder late in 1975, recovered in time to play in the 1975 Pan American Games and the final qualifier in January 1976. I also went with the team on a Soviet Union tour that June.

If it wasn't obvious to me my skills were eroding, it was obvious to others.

Later in 1976, I agreed to coach our Junior National Team, my first exposure to international coaching. We trained the team in Las Cruces, New Mexico, and the USVBA was finally allotting some money for training purposes. Even there our 1984 team was taking shape. Dusty Dvorak was one of my setters and Craig Buck — the youngest and most inexperienced player at the time — was with us, too. So were Rod Wilde and Mike Blanchard.

I was named coach of the National Team in late 1976, after a bizarre selection and acceptance process. I don't remember much about the questioning during the interview, except that it was organized by Val Keller, a rather dour guy. Keller had been technical director of the Canadian Volleyball Association for several years. He was hired by the USVBA as our technical director in another effort to upgrade the national level programs and coaching certification.

My interview for the job was held at a Los Angeles airport hotel and was concluded rather late at night. When it was finished, I went down to my room to sleep.

Around midnight, or a little before, Keller woke me and told me I was hired as National coach. I was drowsy when he called, but I don't think Keller was very enthusiastic about the selection. When he finally got around to offering congratulations, the first thing he told me was "You were lucky to be selected, since you gave such a lousy interview." What a terrific act of confidence by the USVBA! "How could you have given such a lousy interview?" he said.

I was kind of dazed, half from sleep, half from what he was saying at that hour. I couldn't figure out what he was talking about.

That was my introduction as National coach. Of course, I gladly accepted, probably with a lot more enthusiasm for the job than was shown for me.

Still, I was near the top of my game and my mindset was as a player. It was tough adjusting to being a coach. I'm sure Pete Rose is now having the same kinds of problems with the Cincinnati Reds. He really wants to continue as a player, but his long-range duties are as manager, and that job takes precedence.

From the committee's perspective, I did have the qualifications. I was a success at Ohio State and had lots of international experience as a player. I had a good rapport with most of the players and had definite ideas about how I wanted to change some training methods. I also had a lot of respect and a strong friendship with Carl McGown, and hoped to carry on some of the principles he had established.

This may appear to be an ego trip, but I think I have always been willing to outwork or outlast anybody or anything standing in my way. I think those traits have been obvious. I'm fairly bright and well educated, and I've had a broad background of experiences.

I also know I wasn't a very good coach when we began our program in Dayton. That, combined with administrative responsibilities, a moderately talented group of athletes, the need to deal with the scope of the entire volleyball community, the new program, and the U.S. pro league made it easy to predict failure. I certainly lived up to that prediction.

It almost ended my coaching career for good.

We performed miserably at the 1978 World Championships and saw no prospects for any significant additions to the team in the near future. I didn't see a light at the end of the tunnel, and was frustrated by all the criticism we were taking.

I decided to become a player again and hand over the coaching duties. Most important to understand, I was not running away from a poor program. But it was obvious we needed maturity. We needed experience. We needed a setter.

I was also motivated by ego. I was still in good shape, a good player, and figured I had the ability to help this team more as a player than as the coach. I hadn't totally adjusted to coaching. My mentality was still directed at playing.

What I did was overestimate my own impact as a player on the team. Certainly I was motivated by my fierce pride and desire to do anything possible to turn the direction of the team around.

Just about everybody counseled me against my decision. McPeak, Neville, and McGown told me I should look to the long term.

"You have to be patient, Doug," McPeak said. "This is not a hurry-up process. Don't tear down in a day what may take a few years to build up."

It is true, I'm not a very patient person. But I believed that the most important change I could make to turn the team into a winning Olympic prospect was to resign and return to playing. I felt I could give the team two needed ingredients: mature leadership, which we lacked, and an addition to our starting lineup.

Although we had capable older players on our team, no one assumed a leadership role, either from a lack of leadership ability or from a lack of acceptance.

As for the needed addition to the team, we had been playing with a 5-1 system using one setter. It hadn't been very successful, which is not a criticism of Dave Olbright, our setter at the time. He was an outstanding player. The system just wasn't working. I was looking for any player who could immediately get into the starting lineup and make a positive change in the team. The only player I knew who could do that was me. (Later, of course, with Dvorak as our only setter, the 5-1 worked well.)

The official resignation came a month or so after the World Championships. I felt the whole thing had to be an inside job, engineered from beginning to end. We certainly couldn't advertise the position or go through a long, protracted search for a new coach.

If a new coach came in and changed the whole program, my desires for maintaining continuity would have been dissipated. I felt that Coleman was the only person who knew our program and could take over the team. He had been my technical advisor since the beginning in Dayton.

He agreed to do it, and left his position at George Williams College in Chicago. Coleman took over in 1979 and I became a player. Unfortunately, nothing else worked out quite as well as the transfer.

When you're the head coach, everything looks a little different. Coleman decided to bring in some younger players, which split the team a little, and he made some tactical changes. In general, though, the failure was really my own. I simply wasn't as good a player as I had thought and didn't make nearly the impact on the team I had hoped for.

We were probably a worse team in the Zone Championships in 1979 than we had been at the World Championships in 1978. We were more inconsistent, more prone to highs and lows, more disorganized on the court. We were a horrendous team and really didn't settle down until after the decision to leave Dayton and move to San Diego.

Going into that tournament, though, Coleman was optimistic. He actually thought we were going to win. Well, we ended up losing a match to the Dominican Republic. How we ever lost to those guys is beyond belief.

A reporter went with us from *Volleyball Magazine*, a publication dedicated to snickering at our failures. We lost to the Dominican Republic and this guy got on the bus with us and ranted and raved about how the Dominican Republic team had been together only about a month and all the players had come out of the sugar cane fields, and how we had just lost to them.

That wasn't all true, of course. That team had been together for quite a while. But he was trying to be demeaning, and succeeded. Nobody said anything back to him. We were too hurt ourselves. And I was going to help this team? We lost to the Dominican Republic!

There was a good part for me, though. When I withdrew from the daily grind of coaching and from administrative work, I had the opportunity to finish my dissertation in the physiology lab at the WSU medical school and step back from the whole situation to evaluate my goals.

That period of time convinced me to coach again, and helped make our program successful once we arrived in San Diego. I suppose if I had to do it all over, I wouldn't resign to become a player. On the other hand, it all worked out well.

I returned, and the team moved. The program, mired in mediocrity, got better. The athletes we attracted were better. It wasn't easy to look forward to 1984 from a 1978 vantage point. But eventually, 1984 arrived, and it was a lot better than any of us ever imagined.

Chapter 10.

1982.
The World Championships.

By 1982, much of our team was set and we were well on our way toward developing our playing system.

After an extended training in San Diego, we had our first competition that year against Canada, playing five matches and winning them all. We felt in control, winning two of the matches in three games and three in five.

Smith was gone, but he hadn't yet filed his grievance. We were also without Hovland, who was back in school. We had no idea he'd never be back. Timmons and Kiraly were also in school, so we were winning without many key players.

On June 18-19, we had a two-day series with Mexico and all our players were back, except for Hovland. We won both matches. It was also around that time that the IVBF gave back amateur standing to players who had participated in the long since defunct pro league.

The pro league ran from 1974 to 1980 and the players really didn't make much out of it. In fact, players today make more money with European club teams that are still considered amateur.

The international powers have no problem with that. Yet it was a big deal to make these players amateur again. There seemed to be two sets of rules.

We took five of the former "pros" and increased our roster to 16. Unfortunately, most of the players who had participated as pros were already past their prime, although we did get lots of good play from Rod Wilde.

The others who joined us were Jay Hanseth, Reede Reynolds, Larry Benecke, and Jon Roberts. Only Roberts had prior National Team experience, back in 1974-75. We also added Chris Marlowe.

After those two days playing Mexico, we left on a trip no one wanted to take, an extended stay in the Orient, from June 22 to August 2. I thought half the team would kiss the ground in San Diego when we got home. Travel can be fun, but home is home and it's hard to stay perfectly sane when you're on the road for so long.

Travel is tough. It means long hours in airplanes, different beds, foreign foods, and different times zones. Another problem for American teams is the change in standard of living. Teams from other countries love to visit the United States because their standard of living usually improves. When we travel, we can't readily find amenities we take for granted. For instance, finding fresh fruit, vegetables, and milk in Bulgaria is nearly impossible. And in some hotels, the hot water can be turned off for half the day.

Usually, we try to limit our tours to two weeks or less. However, when traveling abroad, we sometimes economize and play as many matches as we can while there.

On the Orient tour, we were invited first to a tournament in China. Our yearly home-and-home series with Japan wasn't supposed to begin until 10 days after the China tournament, so rather than go home and fly back, we scheduled matches in Korea.

The longer the tour lasted, the crazier we became. One moment we would be serious, the next like circus clowns and cutups. Our normal routine was broken up once, when we found some softball equipment and played a game in Korea, where baseball and softball are extremely popular.

As for our volleyball, we made progress.

In Shanghai we won six of nine matches, losing to China twice and Brazil once, all in five games. We beat a strong French team 3-1, and beat Yugoslavia 3-1. Even though we lost to China, we felt we were at least even with them. One match was on Chinese television, so I suppose 200 to 300 million people saw us lose, and were happy.

The match we lost to Brazil had its share of controversy. If we had problems adhering to international protocol, Brazil had even more problems. They screamed and yelled at officials all night. I never understood how other teams could do that and play well. Every time we argued and complained, we fell apart. Yet Brazil, using a volatile group of players, was masterful at that kind of behavior. But this time, they went a little too far.

There were about 20,000 fans in the stands and we won the first two games, 15-6, 16-14. We were leading 9-1 in the third game when Brazil began holding up play. I don't know if they were serious or if it was just a ploy to throw us off. There were so many delays in the match, the tempo changed and all of a sudden we lost the third game, 15-10. Then we lost 15-5. In the final game, we were up 12-6, but lost 15-12.

The distractions seemed to do us in. It was so bad that the Brazilians were reprimanded by the referee and even the president of the International Volleyball Federation, Frenchman Paul Libaud. But it was too late to help us.

Libaud reprimanded the Brazilian team privately, then publicly in front of all those fans. The unprecedented display by the Brazilian team drew an unheard-of response.

At that time we tried to use both Dvorak and Kiraly as setters. Dvorak, though, wanted to set alone, and Kiraly said that was okay with him. After that tournament, Kiraly never set again, even though that would have been a good two-setter situation for us. We just couldn't get Dvorak to go along.

We finished third in the tournament, although we thought we were the best team. If not the best, then second best.

After the tournament, we stayed for one more exhibition with China, which we also lost in five games. I remember it well because I believe it was the only time I've ever seen Berzins yellow-carded. We had received some bad calls, and once when Berzins went back to serve, he was so angry he slammed the ball down so it bounced at least 40 feet.

That's when he got the yellow card. We had a rule that if a player did something unprovoked, he would be removed from the game. We took Berzins out immediately, even though he had been playing well, and we promptly lost the last two games.

Real good coaching. But we have to deal with bad calls. It's part of the game.

Next up was our trip to Korea, and we played in Seoul, where the 1988 Games will be held. We won a small tournament easily, beating Korea twice, and weak teams from India and Canada. We probably beat Canada more times in more places over the years than any other team. And Canada was developing a good team, too. We closed our Korean stay with a couple of exhibition wins.

Then it was time to go to Japan, although if I had said, "Let's go back to San Diego," there would have been a stampede for the airport.

We lost the first match 3-0, which helped to shake us up. We won three of the next six matches easily and could have won a couple more. It was the first time we had beaten Japan there, so it was a major breakthrough.

Japan wasn't the easiest place to play. Not only were we far from home, but the Japanese aired their matches on television. Since they play according to the television schedule — just like here in the United States — the matches were played in the afternoon, and we traveled at night. Our players adjusted, though. One of our strengths is the ability to sleep in any condition, under any situation, in any cramped quarters.

Our team could eat, sleep, read, and shop in addition to playing volleyball well. I could never understand how a guy could come in one day begging for $100 to stay afloat, then load up on unbelievable quantities of stereo equipment in Japan, supposedly for relatives. Books were also big on the trips and were handed around for all to read. On this particular trip, nutrition books were of most interest, and anyone caught eating sugar was sternly reprimanded by the others.

Duwelius was outstanding on that trip, among others. Powers wasn't back with us yet, and Buck didn't go because of shoulder surgery. We were still using a three middle-blocker system and trying to get ready for the World Championships in Argentina in October.

All our training, the Orient tour, and the series that followed, were in preparation for those Championships.

When we returned from the Orient on August 2, we began a five-match domestic tour in the Midwest with the Italian team. The Italians were mediocre then, but improved enough to win the bronze medal at the 1984 Olympics.

Most of our starting players were left at home during this trip — we owed it to them for what they did in the Orient — so it didn't bother us as much when we lost two of the five matches. Dvorak, Waldie, Sunderland, and Buck didn't play, and Kiraly was injured in the first match. Winning three of the matches was a plus.

During this tour we began to look closely at Wilde and Marlowe, and it became apparent they would be competing for the same position. Crabb had joined the coaching staff at that time, and we accomplished much as far as determining our players' abilities.

Our next tour was with Korea. They had a significant addition to their team, Kang Man-Soo, a great outside hitter. We played one very bad match, but won all four of the others on that tour.

Still, we were not as consistent in 1982 as we had been in 1981. On our better days, we were better than in 1981; but on our average days, we were much worse.

Our last match with Korea was on September 12 at Sacramento State College. Korea won only four points in the last two games. It was demoralizing for them.

We thought we were competitive with anybody now, and our final World Championships prep series was against Poland in late September. Poland had a long history of being a great team. They had won the gold medal at the 1976 Olympics, upsetting the Soviets. We had six matches, and it would be a major test for us, a benchmark of how good we were.

When the series began in Wichita on September 19, our coaching staff was unimpressed with the Poles, but our players were still a little in awe of them. They let it affect their play and we were crushed. The next match was in Provo, Utah, and we won, 3-1, in front of my former coach, McGown. It was fun to win in front of him so he could take some satisfaction in having helped the program along. Carl is particularly fond of the Poles, yet he never coached a victory over them.

In Provo, McGown housed us in a Brigham Young University dorm, which might have been his little joke on the Poles. BYU has stern rules against smoking, drinking, and general rowdiness in the dorms, and the Poles are world class on all three counts. When we all checked in and were read the rules, the looks on their faces had our team laughing up our sleeves.

Another of the matches in the Long Beach Arena, was an emotional victory in front of a crowd of about 6,000 noisy fans. That's quite a bit below capacity, but the crowd was really behind us and we could all visualize the Olympics. We got a pre-Olympic tingle.

The Polish tour ended 3-3 in matches, although we won more games. We felt we had established a strong trend going into the World Championships, our most important competition in the four-year period other than the Olympics. The championships came at about the time of the Falkland Islands incident and we couldn't be certain we'd go to Argentina. There was a possibility of the tournament being called off, or of our trip being canceled by the State Department.

Despite the Falkland incident, the Championships were not canceled or postponed. And we went knowing we wouldn't be popular. For some reason, Canada was less popular. I guess because there was no British team there, making Canada a good substitute.

We had some garbage thrown at us from the stands, but a couple of times the crowds had to be hosed down to keep from storming the Canadian team. It was nasty. In foreign countries, they don't boo when they don't like something like we do here. They whistle. When we played, it was pretty shrill.

The Soviets, and Bulgaria and Chile were in our pool. We had to finish first or second to be one of the top 12 teams. Chile would be no problem, but we had to beat one of the other two teams.

The trip was memorable. We had a 12-hour flight — what's a few hours when you're having fun — with a couple of stops on the way. It was an all-night ordeal, and when we finally landed in Buenos Aires, it was about 6 a.m. the next day. We were all looking forward to a little sleep.

Unfortunately, Buenos Aires wasn't where we were going to play. So the welcoming committee met us at the airport and told us we would be put up in a hotel to rest, then brought back to the airport to fly to Catamarca, our ultimate destination, later that afternoon.

This plan seemed workable, but the hotel wasn't ready for us and the committee decided to take us on a tour of the city.

Now Buenos Aires is a beautiful city, very European, but the last thing we wanted to do was take a tour. We spent about three hours on a bus, but I don't think anyone saw much. They were all sleeping.

When we finally pulled into the hotel, the rooms still weren't ready, so they offered us a meal. All anyone really wanted to do was get some sleep, but we had no alternative. We ate.

After only a few hours in the rooms, we were taken to the airport, again by bus, and by now the traffic was a joke. We finally made it to the airport, but after the hour-and-a-half flight we weren't even close to Catamarca. We were herded onto another bus — this one a converted school bus, not anything like an American Greyhound — for a seven-hour ride. I've got to give the guys a lot of credit for this one. They all found a way to sleep.

I usually can't sleep on a bus so I sat up in front with the driver and our Argentine interpreter, Alehandro. Alehandro made some local traditional tea and I'm not sure what was in it. Anyway, he had a thermos with boiling water and made some strong, vile stuff. Since it was the only thing available, I drank about five cups. No way was I going to sleep after drinking that.

We didn't get to Catamarca until approximately 2 a.m., and from all we could see, it was a real podunk town up near the Andes. I couldn't understand how they filled the stands of the arena every night. There didn't seem to be enough people in town to attend the matches. They must have lived out on farms.

The arena was in the middle of town and was semi-open. In the very dry and dusty climate, that meant we'd arrive for practice sessions in the morning and have to mop the floor before we could play. A fine layer of dust was everywhere.

The arena seated nearly 6,000 people and had good lighting and facilities. But we were not the most popular team in Argentina. No crowd support at all.

I was proud of my team under the circumstances. I thought we handled the situation well. We never played a bad match, even under the worst of conditions.

We developed some stomach disorders but couldn't run out to pick up some Vibramycin, which we had forgotten to bring along. You can play with a stomach disorder, but usually without much stamina. That's what happened to Duwelius, and he had taken over for Waldie, who had a sprained ankle.

We drew Bulgaria for our opening match on October 2. With both scouting reports and confidence, we thought we had an advantage. We knew how strong they were, but they didn't know how strong we were. Our team had.changed a lot since they last saw us, not only in personnel, but in tactics. We thought they'd be surprised at how much we had improved.

We lost, 3-2, in a three-and-a-half hour match. The score of the final game was 16-14 after we had been up 12-5. In addition to Waldie being hurt and Duwelius sick, I made some lineup substitutions that didn't work as planned. I took Buck out and should have kept him in late in the fifth game. I used Duwelius more than necessary instead of Blanchard. Unless we could recoup and beat the Soviets, our best finish would be 13th instead of 5th or 6th.

This was a match we won in every way but on the scoreboard.

It was an enormous disappointment, but it would be the last time Bulgaria would beat us for a long time.

Now, we had to face the Soviet Union. One of the toughest things in sports is to forget about a match almost won and concentrate on the next one. The next match was against the reigning World Champions.

Waldie made an effort to play, but was clearly not capable. Duwelius was still sick. We lost, of course. Our only consolation was that we scored more points than anyone else against the Soviets, losing 15-11, 15-12, 16-14. I was so drained, I sent Neville to the press conference. He's such a feisty guy, he said we'd beat the Soviet Union the next time we played and said some other things that made it sound as if we were a little bitter. We didn't get much good press out of that.

We did finish 13th, never being pressed hard the rest of the way. Our second pool remained in Catamarca; then we moved on to Mendoza, a nice city. Fortunately, we were able to fly the whole way in a small military transport. It was much better than a bus ride.

We beat Chile, Libya, Venezuela, Iraq, Rumania, France, and Italy, losing only one game, to Rumania.

Our consolation for finishing 13th was knowing that in 1978, under similar conditions, we couldn't have beaten any of those teams.

We returned from Argentina with Japan. Japan had finished fourth in the World Championships. We thought their high finish had more to do with the tournament's draw than their ability. We wanted to use this domestic tour to show ourselves where we rightfully belonged.

We won all five of our matches.

Our final competition of 1982 was at the Canada Cup, where we sent a weakened team. Still, we beat a club team from Canada, then Japan, but lost to the Canadian Nationals in the finals, 3-2. We figured the year ended on the upswing.

This was the period of time we were planning our Outward Bound trip. We also had talked in Argentina about making some changes in our style of play. I had McGown and Ken Preston (the coach from Santa Barbara) in Argentina in addition to Neville and Crabb. We did so much analysis and tactical theorizing that by the conclusion of the tournament, we could beat any team in the world on paper 3-0 every time out. And our analysis paid off. The changes we made as a result made us almost unbeatable by the end of 1983.

Chapter 11.

Outward Bound.
And we thought Dayton was cold.

I don't think we would have attempted an exercise the scope of Outward Bound had we put together a close-knit team of players who truly cared about and respected each other.

Team cohesiveness is certainly a necessity, but our first interest had been ability. We could tell early that this group was athletically talented. But they were so independent in background, they had trouble accepting each other. Also, they were all highly educated — free thinkers — and many couldn't accept even the simplest command without raising questions and analyzing motives.

I think there are two kinds of players. The first kind blindly accepts what the coach says. The second starts from the other side and the coach has to justify everything to him. Unfortunately, we had a lot of the second kind.

As far back as the fall of 1980, when we screened applicants for our team, Neville mentioned to me that some of the players were not going to make it on attitude alone. We might even have to sacrifice one or two. A couple of those who obviously didn't make it were Smith and Hovland. A couple of other players were close.

It became obvious that we needed to learn to rely on each other, to develop cohesiveness and relationships that would lend themselves to team play.

Our team had broken down too many times in stressful situations, had allowed too many big leads to get away. If that occurred in the Olympics, it would be ruinous.

Before our team gathered in San Diego, I discussed the proposed team members with our two psychologists, Dr. Don Murray and Dr. Chuck Johnson, who specialized in group dynamics, and we decided that the players needed to share a significant life experience to blend them together.

Just how that would be possible was unknown and it took up much meeting time and discussion. We kicked around all kinds of ideas, some of them wild. Other than playing volleyball with each other for three years or more, our players, so different from each other, had shared little. This project had to be distinctive, something unique to sports.

None of us had heard of Outward Bound — that is, before Neville joined in on the meetings — but we knew we wanted something that would force our players to rely on one another, something only a little less demanding than being in an Army combat zone.

The Army, though, did have some appeal. We actually contacted Camp Pendleton to see if we could put our men through boot camp for a week or so. Pendleton wasn't too crazy about the idea, and the more we thought about it, we weren't either.

We also considered holding an elaborate fraternity-like rush hazing that would last a week or 10 days, but we weren't sure we could find enough peanut butter, or that this was different enough from the players' normal behavior.

When Neville finally joined us in San Diego, Murray, Johnson, and I explained to him what we wanted. I assigned him the task of finding a suitable "life experience."

Neville had extensive outdoor camping and backpacking training and knew about Outward Bound. He wrote the main school in Connecticut to find out if they would be interested in designing a program specifically for us.

The project was passed on to the Colorado school of Outward Bound, and we were on our way.

Outward Bound normally deals with businessmen or students to help them "learn to draw on the best in themselves in times of challenge and decision." The concept originated in World War II England and was designed to instill confidence and strength of character in young merchant seamen who daily faced the prospect of being thrown adrift in the North Atlantic.

Today the program doesn't deal so much with life and death situations as it does with teaching people strong habits of cooperation and responsibility. Students learn to trust and be trusted.

That sounded like what we had in mind. We wanted to make sure the course we took was difficult enough to push our players, but not so difficult they wouldn't gain anything out of it at all.

We needed a unifying experience, so players would learn to get along off-court, as well as on. Then, if things went badly during a game, they would pull together instead of trying to tear each other apart.

We wanted to create a situation that would cause personal values assessment, tap deep inner resources, and require strong, crisp decision making.

Most of the Outward Bound programs are designed for summer participation, but since most of our players were all too familiar with summer activities, Outward Bound suggested a winter experience.

Few of our athletes had ever experienced sleeping on ice, dealing with inclement weather, winterizing a house, or digging a car out of the snow. The climate in southern California isn't like that. Going for a ski vacation isn't even like that. On a lot of those slopes, the snow isn't real.

Our team had to learn patience, tolerance, and acceptance of others' faults, and to remain positive even under the most dire circumstances.

The reaction to our trip was expected. Nobody wanted to go. We had numerous formal meetings on the issue and had to provide proof of Outward Bound's safety record, assuring the players that nobody was going to die. The majority rebelled so vigorously about going that we backed down a bit, and cut the course from 28 to 21 days. We went to great lengths to satisfy all doubts.

Their reaction was typical of what we were trying to eliminate. The players didn't trust the staff. We respect their education, but one of the keys to a successful team is that members do as they're told. All along our players questioned decisions we made, regarding the makeup of the team or new tactics to be used during matches. Those are segments of a program that just can't be questioned by players.

While we were in Japan during the summer of 1982, Murray was with us. The dates had to be finalized for Outward Bound, so the players made one last plea. They wanted a meeting. Not just a regular meeting. A special meeting. A final meeting.

While this issue was bigger than most, we certainly didn't want to go through this process on every decision we made. For Outward Bound, however, the stakes were higher. We tried to underplay what we were doing, but the players were having none of that. Everyone gathered and we went around the whole room. Murray tried to soft sell it. Neville made his pitch about safety and need.

Finally, three or four of the players said, "Let's do it." I specifically remember Duwelius taking the attitude that we were going to go through with it anyway, so why not just make the most of it?

Only one player didn't go — Kiraly. Some of the others weren't happy about that. Kiraly was in pre-med at UCLA and he was taking his courses in sequence. If he dropped out in the middle, he would have to begin all over again in a year. That wouldn't have been fair to him.

We agonized over that decision for some time and there was much concern on the team about it, but there wasn't much we could do. Unofficially, our Outward Bound trip then became known as "The March Without Karch." Sometimes that was said jokingly, but often there was some bitterness attached, too.

The guys weren't happy, but at least there was some humor involved.

The decision to go did not abate the grumbling, however. At the World Championships, I sat down with some of the older players — Sunderland, Waldie, and Marlowe in particular. I felt they'd have the most influence on the others, and I tried to win their support to waylay any other resistance. From then on, we didn't have a major problem, although the grumblings never stopped, even in the snow of the Utah Canyonlands.

Some of the guys actually went in with good attitudes. They thought if it would help the team, they'd be willing to take a chance. Later, some of our guides let us know the team members realized they weren't particularly close and admitted privately they wished the situation would change. It did change, not spectacularly, but at least enough for us to function as a cohesive unit.

Until that time, during matches in critical situations laced with stress, we occasionally broke down and blamed each other or the officials.

That wasn't stress compared to what we went through on Outward Bound. We traveled nearly 100 miles, by snowshoes mostly, carrying 70-pound packs. We also climbed to 11,000 feet. In the end, we decided the trip was worthwhile.

In all, 15 players took part in the project, including Wilde, Blanchard, Jon Roberts, and Larry Benecke, none of whom played in the Olympics.

Of course, our coaching staff went along, too, as well as Johnson and four guides from the school.

Outward Bound underwrote the entire trip and was involved not only financially, but in respect to its reputation as well. Any success or failure would reflect directly on the school.

Certainly there were additional risks in this program besides those dealing with players' feelings. The staff's major fear focused on injuries. We didn't need Dvorak or Berzins falling off a cliff or spraining an ankle. We were also losing three weeks of valuable conventional training time, and possibly more.

On Friday, January 7, our trip began. We boarded a plane in San Diego and were served breakfast on our way to Denver. Then we transferred planes and headed for Grand Junction, Colorado, near the Utah border on the western slope of the Rocky Mountains.

Quickly, we realized this was no ordinary tour. Before we knew it, we were in the Abajo Mountains and Canyonlands of southeastern Utah.

And we still didn't know what we were getting into. Showers? Are you kidding? It was an adventure just going to the bathroom. One of the guys wanted to know who was carrying the toilet paper. There was no need for it — there was snow.

We were packed with all the equipment we could carry, including extra long sleeping bags. Our packs were supposed to weigh about 70 pounds, but by the end of each day, that seemed like a fraction of their true heft.

We stayed a night in Grand Junction and had a meeting with two of our guides — Peter O'Neil and Randy Udall — who tried to prepare us for the ordeal. The next day we bused to nearby Monticello, Utah, where the rest of the OB staff met us, standing in two feet of snow. It would only get deeper.

It became a standing joke that the next set of tracks we followed would be downhill, but it never seemed to be that way.

The program had five parts or experiences, including The Alpine experience, Resupply, Rock Climbing, Solo, and Finals. There was also a Last Day Exercise.

The Alpine experience was an extremely physical ordeal with a focus on technical skills. We were in two groups and, by necessity, had to become efficient in daily chores related to camp and travel. That wasn't easy. Everyone was looking out for himself in the first day or so, until we realized working together would make it much easier for everyone. The grumbling over doing those tasks was monumental. Eventually, though, everyone channeled their energies toward getting the job done, which was our purpose in the first place.

Along with O'Neil, Udall (whose father, Mo Udall, is a U.S. Congressman from Arizona), Jimbo Buickerood, and Eddie Young guided us through during our three weeks. Buickerood and Young were especially nice on the first day when we drove up in our bus. They pounded us with snowballs.

Oh, yes, this would be fun.

We had roller coaster emotions on that trip. The down side included crossing the windswept, bitter cold North Creek Pass in the Utah mountains and climbing North Peak — which never came; the upside was arriving in camp and finding water, taking off our packs, and knocking back some hot "brew." We tested self-discipline and control under stress, fatigue, and emotional upheaval. There is no question emotions were upheaved.

On the second day, Buck tripped and ran into a tree, suffering a compound fracture of his right snowshoe. On the fourth day, a "slight map-reading error" meant we spent about two hours going downhill in knee-deep powder through an overgrown spruce jungle — in the wrong direction.

The highlight of that particular adventure was my fall. I snowballed about 30 feet, and vividly remembered falling off a cliff overlooking Lake Erie when I was a youngster.

It was a little scarier than an amusement park ride, but a good release for our players after they realized I wasn't hurt. If we hadn't been so far out of our way, I probably wouldn't have fallen. We didn't know how deep the snow was where I fell. Yet as soon as it was determined I was okay, there was a rush to get out cameras for pictures of the "human snowball."

And we didn't think this would be fun.

By the sixth day, we were rock climbing in the Chippean Rocks. It contrasted with the drudgery of snowshoeing over hill and dale with our packs. Climbing also challenged the players' athletic ability, something they always enjoyed.

Surprisingly, Buck was one of the better climbers even though his 6-8 frame didn't lend itself to such agility.

When we met at resupply, we were able to reflect on what we accomplished and what we might want to change for the remainder of our time together. For one thing, our two groups hardly ever intermixed and our original intention was to bring the team together. At the resupply, we were together and talked about the competition between the two groups while sharing each one's experiences. Our emphasis had shifted to problem solving, communication, analysis of respect and self-awareness, and the mixing of the total team. We had several good meetings then.

Just getting to resupply was quite a chore. We were told we were making good time, covering as much as eight miles a day. Then we found out to stay on schedule, we had to travel 25 miles in two days.

Camp Pendleton was sounding a little better. Maybe we should have pressed harder for it.

We forged ahead and covered 16 miles in one day, arriving at what we thought was our campsite well after dark. As it happened, we were well past where we should have stopped, and tempers were shortening.

The day was not without humor, however. In woods along the way, leading into a windswept and desolate meadow, one group had left a note.

"Earth creatures," the note read. "Space shuttle should arrive momentarily. Wait here. If, for some reason, you should not be quickly and conveniently transported to the destination of your choice, ring bell."

We laughed so we wouldn't cry.

There was another nice touch to the "16-miler." Johnson and Marlowe had lagged behind. The others waited for them to catch up so they wouldn't get lost. Finally, we were cooperating.

Once we arrived at resupply, two incidents tested the strength and organization of the program. First was the tragic news of an accident in Hawaii involving Crabb's nephew. Initial word of the accident actually arrived at the Outward Bound office in Colorado on January 13, yet after a series of decisions, Crabb was not told until the morning of the 16th, when he immediately left and headed for Hawaii. There was no question he needed to be informed and needed to be with his family during this painful time, but logistics was a problem.

The Outward Bound personnel waited to relay the information and we waited an extra evening for several solid reasons. Had we been informed on the 13th, the only way to pick up Crabb would have been by helicopter, a dangerous effort. When we actually found out on the night of the 15th, at resupply, we could have told him, but his leaving would have required a long, dangerous and nearly impossible truck ride at night.

On the morning of the 16th, after Crabb had slept restfully, when there was adequate light and transportation, he was told. Telling him immediately would have served no purpose.

We thought we handled the situation as well as possible, but recognized the anguish he felt. It was difficult to weigh the danger against the need to reach a loved one in trouble.

The other incident involved Dvorak. Still much against the trip and looking for a way out, he came up with a story he thought would get him released and able to ride back to the base camp in the resupply truck with Crabb. We asked him to explain to the rest of the team his reason for leaving. We also told him we could not guarantee we would keep his position open on the team. He reconsidered and stayed. He also became more positively involved.

For the Solo experience, each group had a different plan. One had specific written assignments, the other did not. With each group doing something different, it allowed for interplay of ideas when the trip was completed.

There was still griping. Some of it was natural, since we took 15 players who knew only 12 would be picked for the final team. But the players who knew they were absolutely solid picks did the most griping. Those who were still fighting for a job were quieter.

There was also the fear we might choose players who hadn't even gone on the trip (in addition to Kiraly) to be on the final team. This was viewed as being unfair, and would have been. We had no serious discussions about doing that.

Johnson, our psychologist, is a roly-poly sort. He called the trip a death march, although it certainly wasn't. He was just out of shape and had a tougher time keeping up. At least the guys treated him well. He was in his fifties and a school teacher, so even in the best weather he would have had trouble keeping up with younger, well-conditioned athletes. But our guys helped him along, which showed they could care if pressed.

Our solo treks through the woods and snow were excellent and just what we were looking for. There was no overt negative reaction, which meant the program was working. It was the exercise the team enjoyed the most.

For the Finals, the men were divided into four groups on set routes. With some minor problems, all the groups eventually made it. Even though we had guides, they let us make our mistakes and corrections so we would be able to learn as much as possible.

Despite unstable weather, the Finals experience provided the best vehicle to attain the team's stated goals for the program. Team members had to work together to survive, and they did.

At one of the campfire meetings on the trip, we tried to drive the point home. The times when it is most difficult to win and most important to cooperate are the times when a team is losing. When everyone is tired and things are going badly, when the day is late and the match is slipping away, that's when a team has to bind together. That's when teamwork customarily collapses and individuals go their own ways. That was the attitude we were trying to change. Sure, a team must lose to learn how to win, but a team must pull together in the worst of situations, too.

For our finish, an orienteering marathon was designed to replace the traditional Outward Bound running marathon, and for our purpose, it was a great alternative. It was physically challenging, required map and compass skills, was interesting, competitive, tactical, suspenseful, and fun.

However, there were two incidents we didn't handle well that underlined the importance of effective communication in stress situations. The orienteering marathon was run in pairs with a specific time limit to find certain "marks." The main rule was for the people in the pairs to stay together.

In two cases, this didn't happen.

Two hours into the marathon, Jon Roberts' knee was hurting and he decided to return to camp, five miles away. Instead of telling his partner, Neville, who was within hailing distance, Roberts just left and Neville proceeded to search another hour and a half before heading back to camp and finding Roberts there.

In the other case, Rod Wilde and Larry Benecke were so zealous about finding all the marks, they separated. They also missed the time limit and accumulated overwhelming penalty points in the competition. When they returned to camp separately, they had to endure some heavy razzing from teammates.

Although we didn't make the best of the experience, it did change the group. In all, it was an excellent activity and went smoothly through cleanup and the final dinner of steaks, potatoes, salad, and brownies.

After we returned to San Diego, I heard from almost every player either directly or indirectly, that they enjoyed the experience and saw some of its value. As a staff, we saw numerous signs that it accomplished what it was supposed to accomplish, although those things are difficult to judge.

Would we have won the gold medal without this trip? Did it help bring the team together, or would there have been the natural evolution anyway?

The players certainly continued to talk about it. There is no way of determining what impact the trip had on us, but given the same set of circumstances, we'd do it again.

I guess that's the ultimate compliment. We had an easy chance to crack at the Olympics but we didn't. Instead, we rose to the occasion.

Chapter 12.

1983.
Qualifying at the Indianapolis Zones.

People who play volleyball in their back yards, on beaches during vacation, or at company picnics don't always understand what the game is really all about. We haven't done a great job educating the American public about our sport, and most people who play don't really know much about it.

It's probably the same with other sports. The guy on a sandlot thinks he knows all there is about playing baseball in the major leagues, until he gets on the field and finds out how different the game is at the highest level.

Many times I've heard volleyball referred to as "hit and giggle." Anybody who watched the Olympics knows this sport is much more than that.

The television networks know it now, because volleyball received some of the highest ratings during the Olympics. Volleyball is growing in popularity in this country.

And when it comes to ranking complete athletes, volleyball players always do well. The sport combines skills needed in other sports, such as basketball and gymnastics. A player has to be strong and quick. He has to have stamina, and he has to be able to think.

He has to be able to jump and make snap decisions. Volleyball will always be played in the back yard, but there is an elite level, too.

In addition to all that, there are decisions to be made in putting together a winning volleyball team, both in personnel and tactics. If being tall were the only criterion, all volleyball players would be 7-footers, but that doesn't even work in basketball. And, just as in basketball, you can't offer the same offense and defense for every play.

That's why during our eight years putting together the 1984 Olympic team, and especially the four years spent at the training center in San Diego, we tried to fit our system to the ability of our players.

It would have been folly to diagram a system and try to work the players into it even if they didn't fit. Babe Ruth hit a lot of home runs, and telling him to try for singles would have been stupid. Also, trying to steal in front of him would have been a waste of time. He was good at what he could do, and that's that.

When it was obvious our best passers were a couple of shorter guys, Berzins and Kiraly, we decided to go with them almost exclusively. There was no need to work with other players on this skill if we could isolate our best people and allow them to concentrate on what they could do best.

Sometimes, what we wanted to do and what the players wanted to do didn't mesh. We couldn't convince Dvorak we needed two setters instead of one, and he performed well by himself. We used one setter.

The setter on a team is the quarterback, the player who controls the offense. We wanted to use Kiraly as a setter on two of six rotations, and use Dvorak on four of six rotations.

Dvorak argued that he worked better when he was in total control, and we let him go at it. It's almost impossible to make a talented athlete perform in a manner opposed to his background, training, or feelings. Certainly we had some concern about injuries — if Dvorak had been hurt, we would have been in big trouble. We would have had more flexibility with two setters. But Dvorak was the Babe Ruth of setters, and he didn't let us down.

Dvorak ended up playing every minute of the Olympics. He was our only player who never came out. A lot of teams play that way, but we had to. We really didn't have anybody else to put in there.

Some of our changes were planned. Some just happened. Even in the year of the Olympics, we made several meaningful changes in our style.

After the 1982 World Championships in Argentina, we began adding several novel approaches to our game. We really altered our basic concept of passing, offense, and blocking at this time.

Ⓢ - SETTERS Ⓗ - HITTERS

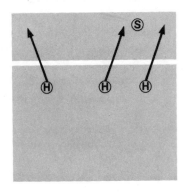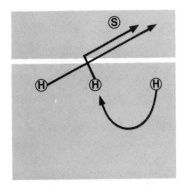

Offense, or Attack Patterns

We had been using a perpendicular offense, running our hitters more or less in straight lines at the net, and we wanted to take advantage of our outside hitters' quickness. We had Kiraly, Sunderland, and Berzins there, and later Saunders. They had good lateral movement, so we decided to change to a more parallel approach to our hitting patterns. That would make it tougher for blockers to follow the hitters' approaches and key into the zone of attack. With perpendicular movement, the blocker sees the hitter all the way. With a parallel, or angled approach pattern, the blocker sees the hitters, but can't tell where the hitter will go. There is much more pressure on the blockers.

We played some rotation defense, never static where everyone holds his position. We wanted Kiraly and Berzins, our best defensive players, to get most of the balls. We moved them to high-probability areas on the floor, in a rotation or slide defense, which was really a key to our team. They were constantly moving toward the area where the ball would likely be hit.

On offense, we started to develop a swing philosophy, really just an extension of the parallel approach concept.

These decisions were not made only by our immediate staff. McGown, Ken Preston, and many others helped us. We wanted as much input as we could get.

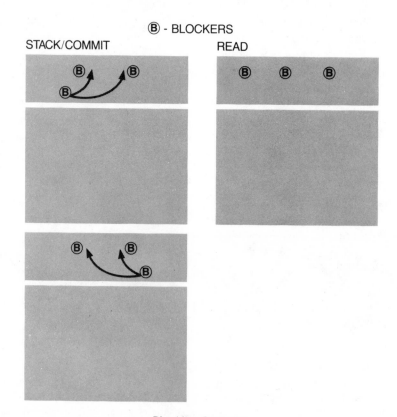

Blocking Systems

In the spring of 1983, we began using our swing hitting attack and also added a new approach to blocking. We had always been a read-and-react team, unsuccessful at stopping most quick attacks in the middle of the court. We needed a combination blocking system that could adapt to different offense systems and give those players with different abilities an opportunity to be successful.

We toyed with three or four blocking systems to find which players were most useful in which system. We began to use a stack system, running our blockers around each other, so we could more easily match up with the quick, combination-type offensive plays.

The Soviets always used the stack, or commit, system and the Poles were always a read-and-react team. We tried to use both. That was significant. No other team in the world was as sophisticated tactically and did as many different things. It enabled us to become a dominating team at the end of 1983 and throughout 1984. It enabled us to put together a successful game plan against any opponent.

We experimented with different rotations. Berzins, for instance, was moved next to Buck, which made Berzins a better offensive player.

We also spent a lot of time studying any match-ups, player by player, with the teams we faced.

Some of our plans were offshoots of plans by famous foreign coaches who had helped us in the early days. The famous Soviet coach, Yuri Chesnekov, taught us a great deal about Soviet systems.

Another coach who helped was Yasutaka Matsudaira of Japan, the international guru of volleyball. From 1963 to 1972, he coached his country's national team in three different Olympics and won successively the bronze, silver, and gold medals. He revolutionized the quick offense, and was the first guy to have players run around each other, change attacking positions, and fake in the air as if they were going to hit. He developed what would be the screen in basketball.

Our tournaments and exhibitions helped develop and hone our systems for the Olympics. After our Outward Bound excursion, we went to Cuba in early April 1983. I thought that would be an important trip for a number of reasons. Cuba is probably the best team for us to train against because it is big and strong and doesn't do a lot of fancy things. The Cubans play straight-up volleyball and would give us good competition.

Powers was back with us by then, and Buck was healthy. Before our trip to Cuba, we had essentially settled on our final team. Now, we wanted to see how well it would play in different situations and with different combinations. We began a two-year polishing process.

The trip to Cuba had its ups and downs. We used our system well, although we were still not comfortable with it, and we lost four of the five matches. Some of the teamwork ideas we were supposed to have learned on Outward Bound had still not taken effect and there was also some grumbling about our system. It was not traditional volleyball, and some of the guys did not want to experiment with new concepts. It takes time to learn new systems, so we weren't too disappointed with the reactions.

Off the court, we became involved with a small production company that was going to film our Cuban tour and use the footage as a promotional film. We were supposed to get $10-15,000 in outside funding for the movie, but that didn't work out. The money eventually came out of our budget.

Worse, the company was having problems getting visas, so we left for Cuba and told them we'd see them in Havana in a couple of days when they were cleared for travel. Naturally, as soon as we arrived in Havana, we found out our matches were going to be played elsewhere. By the time we returned to Havana, the production company people were finally there — after spending eight fun-filled days sunning themselves in Miami waiting for the visas — and they filmed our final match, which we lost. They got the whole thing. We had to change the script. We had to spend more money than we'd planned. We had to look at their tans. It was a bad deal all around. We eventually got a nice film — only the price was too high.

Our roster included everyone we would eventually take to Los Angeles except for Kiraly, who was still in school. But he was almost ready to rejoin us.

After that tour, we played four rather insignificant matches — winning them all — against Canada. Marlowe was left at home and Wilde went with us. In Cuba, the only match we won was with Wilde setting, and we first saw that he had a chance to make the team, although we were about a year away from making a decision on him.

The most important competition of the 1983 season was approaching, and we were confident. We wanted to win the Zone Championships, held in Indianapolis.

Indianapolis has become quite a sports city. It has developed several facilities for both amateur and pro sports, and they are all first class. We played our volleyball matches in Market Square Arena, where the NBA Pacers play.

Although we had already qualified for the Olympics by virtue of being the host team, that wasn't the way we wanted to be accepted. We wanted to earn our way into Long Beach Arena.

Before those Zones, we had an important preparation trip to Europe, playing four matches in Finland and five in Poland. We could have played the Soviets, too, but wanted to wait until we perfected our new tactics. We saw no point in playing the best team in the world, taking the chance of being beaten badly, losing our confidence, and ditching our system.

We also didn't want to peak too soon. We chose Finland because they most closely resembled the Cuban team in size and strength. By now we had our new passing formation, eliminating the big blockers from passing or receiving serves, and putting the passing responsibility on the shoulders of Berzins, Kiraly, and Sunderland.

It was not revolutionary that we were using only two players to receive serve, but it was unusual that they were the same two — Kiraly and Berzins mostly.

Berzins and Kiraly, and sometimes Sunderland and Saunders (when the other two were not in the lineup) essentially passed all the balls. Revolutionary, maybe, but it worked for us. Technically, it was the biggest change we made. If

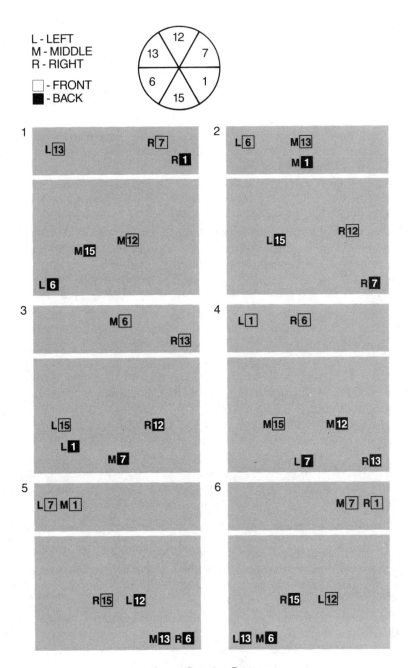

Serve Receive Patterns

anyone else passed a ball during that time to the Olympics, it was usually a mistake.

Passing is the most important part of the game because it sets up the rest of a team's attack, and we were changing accepted passing patterns. Most teams received serves with five guys, or four. We were using two.

Our practices became more like football practices. Quarterbacks over here, kickers over there, linemen in another place.

A segment of the game requiring a great deal of practice now took almost no practice time for the bulk of our team. We didn't have to worry about it because we had specialized that part of our game and also were developing the best pair of pass receivers in the world.

Our technique worked so well, I don't think we were outpassed, except occasionally, the rest of 1983 or 1984. It was an unusual specialization and it's difficult to overplay its success for us.

Eventually, our players became used to our system and although the coaches were comfortable with it all along, it began to work even better than we'd planned. Good personnel always helps a good plan.

In Finland, we won all four of our matches and only two went the full five games. In Poland, we greeted a team that had changed coaches since last we met. Hubert Wagner, the man who had coached the team to the 1976 gold medal, was in charge again, and his team was considered the only major threat to the Soviet Union.

Our first match was played in Katowice, Poland, and we met the challenge. On the first night we won in five games. It was a big victory because it meant we were one of the top teams in the world. We had beaten a very good Polish team on its home ground.

It was an exciting time for us, a highlight of 1983.

We would get better. We went to Indianapolis without Timmons, who went to the World University games, and Wilde was also left at home. Blanchard was the only player who went who didn't play in the Olympics. Berzins had developed into a starter and was becoming increasingly important. We were smooth and dominating. We played almost as well as we could have.

During the Zones, we didn't come close to losing a match. We didn't even lose a game. We dominated Cuba in the final, 15-8, 15-5, 15-6, although the Cubans did not send their entire first team. We also beat Puerto Rico, Canada, Netherlands Antilles, and Mexico. Sunderland played a super Zones —easily his peak performance. It was great to see someone who had given so much perform so well, especially in front of the U.S. crowd.

The Zones field was not quite at full strength because Cuba had already qualified for the Olympics and did not have to qualify again. Canada was tired from the recently completed University games. But I don't think any of those teams were capable of beating us under any circumstances by that time.

The final finish was us, Canada, and Cuba, 1-2-3. That meant Canada qualified from the Zones, since both the United States and Cuba already had spots in Los Angeles. It had been 10 years since we won the Zones, and if we hadn't been the host Olympic team we would have qualified in Indianapolis, a more legitimate way to reach the Games. It certainly was a good feeling.

From there we played a three-match Friendship Tour with Bulgaria, and got some revenge for the World Championships by winning all three matches, losing only two games. The tour went to Montana and San Diego.

Our next test came just two days later and it had more to do with off-court than on-court preparation. We held a Pre-Olympic Quest for Gold tournament in Long Beach, inviting Brazil, Argentina, Japan, Bulgaria, and Canada. This tournament has become traditional, if not mandatory. The host Olympic team holds a pre-Olympic tourney in the Olympic arena a year before the Games.

What should have been a pleasant time was intense because of the Hovland case. And it didn't help that Hovland and some of his friends showed up to watch us play.

After we beat Japan, Argentina, and Canada, we lost a five-setter to Japan in the finals, losing badly in the last game.

We should have dominated that team, and didn't. It was disappointing even though Japan did have a good team. We were tired and had been pointing to playing Brazil in the final, but the Brazilians unexpectedly lost to Japan.

Brazil was becoming a hot and cold team. We were learning something about Brazil that became more obvious when they lost to Korea in the Olympics, even though they were a better team. That team must have had some of the same problems we had in focusing on the matter at hand instead of something down the road.

We did earn some respect by beating Argentina, which had finished third in the World Championships.

After that tournament, we split the team, sending the top eight players to the Soviet Union (now we were ready for them) for the Savvine Tourney, and the rest of the team to the Pan Am Games. We filled in both our rosters with college players. Our team at the Pan Am Games did well, although Brazil won the tournament. We did get some good information on them, though. The tournament was also a turning point for Timmons. He was starting to perform.

In the Soviet Union, our team continued to play the way it had in Indianapolis, although we lost to the Soviets, 3-1. Kiraly had the stomach flu and didn't play. I might have used him had I known it would be our only chance against the Soviets. I misinterpreted the schedule and thought we'd be able to play them again.

Still, it was increasingly evident we were closing the gap, and we got an outstanding report on the Soviets, too, while finishing a strong second in this very prestigious tournament.

We beat Poland, Czechoslovakia, and Finland, all 3-0. Then we beat Japan 3-2, in a very long match. We felt wonderful. We had a strong starting lineup, although we later replaced Salmons with Timmons. Sunderland had to undergo ankle surgery after this tournament, but Powers replaced him well.

Two weeks later we went back to Japan, where we had never won a tour. This one was split, 3-3, but when we put our best team on the floor, we were better.

By the end of October, we were back home playing Poland again, and won five of five matches. We felt we had progressed to the point where we were better than anyone but the Soviets, and we were even with them.

On our way to the Canada Cup in Montreal, we witnessed the only political defection I can remember in my international career.

We left from Newark, and when we got to Montreal, there was a guy missing.

"Hey, you're a man short," I said to one of the Poles.

"Yes, he stayed in America," the man said. It turns out the guy defected. He was their volleyball referee, and apparently nobody cared that he defected. They began making jokes that he was a bad official, anyway. What happened to all the intrigue I used to read about? This guy obviously wasn't in the same league as the Soviet Union's Arkady Shevchenko.

The Canada Cup in Montreal was our last competition of the year and we beat Cuba in the finals after losing to them in the first round. We also beat Poland twice and Canada, losing only one game.

Cuba won the first-round match 3-0, although it was a long match. We met the Cubans again in the final, winning our last two games easily, the final one while allowing only one point.

Kiraly was great during that tournament and was named MVP. He and Dvorak were named to the All-Tournament team.

We were still having trouble getting Buck to perform consistently well and push himself in practice, so one day I took him behind a curtain and yelled so loud not only all the players in the building heard what I said, but about half the people passing by heard, too.

In the final against Cuba, he played one of the great matches of his life. Buck often responded this way. Pushed, he was an outstanding player. Working hard, as hard as a Saunders or a Blanchard, turns Buck into a premium player.

We were content, though. We had ended 1983 in great shape and were fired up for 1984.

Our results over the years kept improving. In 1977 we had won only 38.5 percent of our matches. In 1981, we won 62.5 percent.

In 1982, we were up to 75 percent of our matches and in 1983, we won 77.4 percent.

It was time for the final push. In 1984, the Olympic year, we won 79.6 percent of all our matches played.

It was quite a record. It was quite a year.

Chapter 13.

1984.
New tactics and the Soviet boycott.

It was 1984 and countdown time — everything had more meaning, everybody reacted a little differently. Matches were more important. Nobody wanted to sit out. Minor injuries seemed to heal more quickly. This was the culmination of what we had been training for, not only in the last four or eight years, but in our lives. It was almost surreal. The year seemed to go in slow motion, but looking back, it slipped by all too quickly.

Our competitive schedule was short. We traded tours with Cuba, going there in early February and having them come here a month later. These were important matches.

We asked the Cubans if we could play our matches in large arenas to better prepare us all for what we would encounter in the Olympics. The Cubans complied beautifully. The matches were played in Havana in a magnificent arena. There was television coverage, and the Cubans could not have been better hosts. We won two of the six matches in Cuba and split a six-match series in our country.

It was significant, though, that we won the second match in Cuba. It was the first victory for us in Cuba in a big arena, and we were still playing around with our lineup.

Years before when we played Cuba, it was a disaster. In 1977, when we were stationed in Dayton, the Cubans came up for a seven-city tour. We didn't win a game — yep, 21-0.

One match was played in Madison, Wisconsin, the radical capital of the world. The whole city welcomed Cuba with open arms. We went to a pro-Cuban rally, and even the Cubans didn't know what to make of it, although they were polite. The city mayor, a young, long-haired-type, got up and started chanting "Cuba for the Cubans." It was bizarre.

At the arena, which was packed, the fans were cheering for Cuba. They had signs and lettered bedsheets they carried around the place. Coleman was with us as an advisor on that trip, and when two guys paraded in front of our bench, Coleman, normally a placid man, jumped up and gave the sign a karate chop, tearing it down the middle.

We were all heavily guarded on that trip, but I think the Cubans were in friendly territory. Madison is known for behavior like that.

Years later, in 1984, Cuba's home crowd didn't demonstrate as much, and we actually had a chance to win. But it was hot out and the sun was shining, a problem for the southern Californians on the roster.

"Don't go out in the sun longer than 15 minutes," I tell the troops.

So the whole team goes out in the sun and Powers falls asleep in a lounge chair with his sunglasses on. He showed up at the match looking like a raccoon. He had to wait until the last minute to put on his jersey. His legs were beet red, his chest was beet red, his face, except around his eyes was beet red, and I was beet red from anger.

It was the third time Powers had done something like that. He didn't play the rest of the trip. I probably did him a favor, saving him from unwanted quick peeling.

After the matches, the staff visited the Old Floridita Tavern where Hemingway spent time. There was a bust of Hemingway in the place and the food was great, especially after all the beans and rice we had been eating. There was even a guy behind the bar who remembered Hemingway. It was something we didn't expect to find there.

We didn't win as many matches as we would have liked, and felt that one of the matches was taken away by the referee in Cuba. That would have made us 3-3.

Salmons was ineffective, and we didn't know why until we discovered a stress fracture in his leg. It was one of those nagging things that kept him out of the lineup almost to the Olympics. Buck, too, was having a problem with his ankle, and needed an operation. Buck's injury gave us the chance to play Timmons. He became irreplaceable. This was the guy we'd been farming out to junior teams.

Relying heavily on Timmons and Duwelius, we did fine, which said something about our depth. We could play any number of players and do well.

There was one other incident in Cuba involving Neville and me. We stayed in a hotel by Embassy Row, on the one street in Cuba that looks like civilization as we know it. The rest of Cuba looks like it's lost in a time warp from the 1920s.

We were jogging along this street and when we got to a corner, a guard stopped us and started speaking rapidly in Spanish. It turned out that earlier in the day one of our delegation members — the head of it no less — had given this guy a hard time. So the police detained us for two hours. We just sat on the curb while the whole thing was being ironed out. No sense giving a guy holding a machine gun trouble.

We won our first match with Cuba on the return trip in Santa Barbara, and won our last two matches with them, allowing us to break even. We knew we were close to them in ability, and the outcome of the 12 matches substantiated this. They won seven of the 12 matches, but only three more games. The difference in total points was 8. Physically, Cuba was stronger than we were, and we figured they would be among our strongest competition — but that was before the boycott was announced.

Our next matches were against Czechoslovakia, giving us an opportunity to play a big, slow European team. Czechoslovakia hadn't qualified for the Olympics, but their team resembled some of the teams that had. It also gave us our first competition without Marlowe. Marlowe had been cut after the Cuban series because Wilde was outplaying him. We had delayed as long as possible in making the cut. We had known that releasing Chris would be hard for the team to take, and we had wanted to go directly into competition so the team could focus on the matches rather than on their disappointment. And we had wanted to give Rod the opportunity to prove his value and to be accepted. There were three matches in the United States, and we won them all. Everybody played.

We then hosted a Championship Series, one big tournament made up of three smaller ones. It was Neville's idea, and proved very successful.

The Czechoslovakian team was still in our country, and the teams from Canada and Japan joined us. Our first match was against Japan, and we humiliated them, 15-1, 15-5, 15-7. That match was aired in Japan, where I'm sure it wasn't received too well.

Volleyball is really the perfect game for the Japanese. The idea is to immerse your identity into the team, and the Japanese were for doing things in groups. The only way to beat the Japanese was to beat them physically — overpower them. Otherwise, they would win, because they did things so perfectly.

By the time we played Canada, we had only two starters left who were completely healthy. Berzins had a groin pull and Kiraly was sick. Powers was benched. We lost in five games, 15-13 in each of the last two. Two days later, the Canadians whipped us again, and decisively at that. That match was played in Santa Barbara on April 2. It was the first time we had lost there, Kiraly's home, and the last match we would lose until Brazil beat us in the round-robin of the Olympic Games on August 6. We went for four months and 25 matches without a loss.

Next up was a four-day vacation in Hawaii where we participated in a fundraiser with Tom Selleck. He played in a match with us.

After that vacation came the highlight of our year to that point — our tour to the Soviet Union. We had been preparing for this confrontation for almost a year. We were going there to see just how good we were, with a two-match stopoff first in Bulgaria, and a small tournament in Czechoslovakia after the Soviet matches. We had no idea how successful we would be when we left, or that we were going to have a bombshell dropped on us after we arrived.

We won the two matches in Bulgaria, gaining revenge for what had happened in the World Championships, even though we didn't play particularly well.

Salmons was still nursing his injury and didn't make the trip, and Buck was not at top strength. He was hobbling around a good deal. One night I took Buck aside and told him we needed him in the lineup and he would just have to play over the pain.

"Look, Craig, if you can't play now, you'll probably miss the Olympics, anyway," I said. "You might as well go all out and see if you can play over the pain. If you can't, it won't be an injury that's going to hobble you for life. If you can play with a little pain, you'll be a great addition to the team."

"All right," he said. "I'll try tomorrow and see how it goes. It's just that I've put in all this time on rehabilitation, and it doesn't seem to me the ankle is any better."

"Everybody at this level plays with some sort of pain," I said. "I think if you try, you'll find you won't even notice."

The next day Buck warmed up and played the whole match. When he discovered how good he could be, even in pain, the look on his face indicated he was celebrating about a thousand Christmases at once. His ankle never bothered him again, at least not enough for him to miss any matches.

Meanwhile, Wilde was playing great volleyball for us under some tough conditions. He was being subjected to quiet abuse by not being totally accepted by the team. Yet every time we put him in, he scored points or created scoring opportunities.

That was the situation when we went to the Soviet Union for matches on May 8, 10, 12, and 13 in Kharkov. The arena was good and so was the weather. It was a nice situation for us. The Soviets were huge and powerful, but also predictable, we thought. Most important, our team believed in its new system and in our ability to win.

We hadn't beaten the Soviet Union in 16 years, not since the 1968 Olympic Games. We were tied 2-2 in the first match when we took a five-minute break in our locker room before the final game. The fourth game had ended in our favor, 16-14, so we were looking for a super finish. I don't think the Soviet players knew what was coming, and I'm certain we didn't.

The boycott, though, was about to be announced.

During that final game, it was obvious something was wrong. It didn't appear the Soviets were playing any differently, but it seemed some of the usual fire was taken out of the coaching staff. I think the staff was told of the boycott before that final game.

I don't know what purpose it served to tell them then, but it was obvious they knew. We thought we were the better team from the second game on, and for the first time, under great pressure, we had won that fourth game. But in the fifth game, the Soviet coach, Vjatcheslav Platonov, didn't seem as intense. He seemed distracted. His players must have sensed something was wrong. We dominated, 15-6.

The year before, when we made a Soviet tour and lost, we were still good enough to impress the officials over there. Victor Amalyin, the director of research for the Soviet Volleyball Federation, who had befriended me on a tour

From top left to right the players are: Aldis Berzins, Mike Blanchard, Craig Buck, Rich Duwelius, Dusty Dvorak, Karch Kiraly, Chris Marlowe, Pat Powers, Steve Salmons, Dave Saunders, Paul Sunderland, Steve Timmons, Marc Waldie, Rod Wilde.

Opposite It's over, we've won, and pandemonium reigns! Marlowe, Powers, Berzins, and I are swept up in the celebration.

Top A more tense time. Dvorak and I share a strategy change early in the Olympics.

Bottom Throughout the games I gave time-out instructions to millions of new volleyball fans.

Bruce Hazelton

Bruce Hazelton

Opposite   Powers could rise to amazing heights and by the end of the Olympics was dominating our opponents.
Top   Buck gets some special instruction during a break in the Gold Medal match.
Bottom   Berzins and Kiraly, our backcourt aces against Tunisia.

opposite Bruce Hazelton

Opposite Steve Salmons tries to turn the tide in our pool match with Brazil. Nothing went quite right that night.

Top The staff that made it happen, perhaps the best ever: (l to r) Beal, Neville, Crabb, statistician Mark Miller.

Bottom Marlowe rushes into my arms shortly after the final point is scored.

Bruce Hazelton

Bruce Hazelton

Bruce Hazelton

Opposite Buck was extremely effective against Korea, even when they committed a blocker to him.
Top A more casual form of coaching.
Middle In our first match with Brazil, their block reacted well to our offense.
Bottom Sometimes we simply need to calm things down. Saunders (#2), Powers (#13), and Timmons get the word during an early Olympics match.

opposite Bruce Hazelton

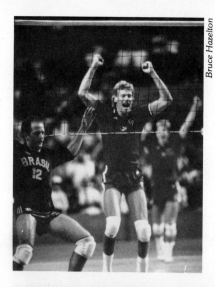

Bruce Hazelton

Opposite Dvorak (#1) and the rest of the team left Tunisia flat footed in one of the quickest matches in Olympic history.
Top Buck reacts to the final point for the Gold Medal. Brazil's Razman (#12) leans on the net in frustration.
Middle Kiraly could get some balls other players never even reacted to.
Bottom Powers (#13) goes for the second half of a well-executed combination play against a confused Argentina in our opening Olympic match.

Bruce Hazelton

Bruce Hazelton

Ron Haase

Bruce Hazelton

Opposite Kiraly was magnificent receiving serve, and he burns with an uncommon intensity.

Top Blanchard (#11) and Timmons (#6) in Cuba in early '84. The team was jelling.

Bottom For Berzins, no position in the backcourt was unnatural. Marlowe (#10) looks on.

Bruce Hazelton

Bruce Hazelton

Opposite Wearing my best smile and having a lot of fun.
Top The middle blockers got some special instruction; here it's Buck, with Timmons (#6) looking on.
Bottom Now it's Timmons' turn, with Powers (#13) adding support.

opposite Ron Haase

Bruce Hazelton

Opposite When Timmons (#6) and Powers kept their eyes open, our blocking improved.
Top The end of a quick combination play to our right side. It worked very well against a disorganized Korean block. Berzins is alone at the net to score.
Bottom Kiraly, a most powerful athelete, plays bigger than his 6′3″ size.

Bruce Hazelton

opposite Jon Hastings

Opposite The snow was deep, the journey was long. I'm glad we have some photos to remind us how beautiful the country was.
Top We look for a campsite as the sun falls.
Middle No beach in site, we push on.
Bottom Timmons leads our psychologist Chuck Johnson. Both look a little fatigued.

Bruce Hazelton

Jon Hastings

Opposite My favorite of Hovland's shots. The beach was his environment, and he's still unhappy.
Top The Brazilians celebrate their pool victory — five days too early!
Bottom Sinjin Smith, hat firmly in place.

opposite Jon Hastings

Bruce Hazelton

Opposite Berzins (#12), Duwelius (#5), and Powers put up a good block against Canada.
Top The Koreans did a great job against us for one game. They deserved better than fifth!
Bottom The unfortunate Rod Wilde delivering a quick set to Steve Timmons during a match in Santa Barbara early in '84.

Tim Ryan

opposite Jon Hastings

Opposite Marc Waldie; perfect form, perfect concentration. A worthy Gold Medalist for the United States. **Top** Sunderland helped us a great deal in the win over a very tough Korean team. **Bottom** Berzins was particularly effective as a hitter because everyone concentrated on stopping Buck. Here Aldis finishes off a crossing pattern against one very late and poorly positioned blocker.

Bruce Hazelton

Bruce Hazelton

oppsoite Dennis Steers

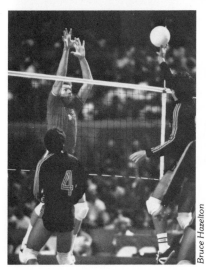

Bruce Hazelton

Opposite   Powers reigned supreme over Brazil for the Gold!
Top   Dvorak had lots of ideas about our offense and team.
Bottom left   Timmons dominated the net during most of '84.
Bottom right   Another perfect pass from Kiraly.

Bruce Hazelton

Opposite The final moment, victory is ours! Kiraly, Buck, and Berzins celebrate.
Top The team is really together now. Berzins tries to pick me up, but he's too weak!
Middle Marlowe — always prepared and always eloquent.
Bottom Our loyal American volleyball supporters — from Japan.

Bruce Hazelton

Bruce Hazelton

Bruce Hazelton

Bruce Hazelton

Bruce Hazelton

Opposite Marlowe — also an unabashed patriot.
Top To the victor belong the spoils.
Middle and bottom Salmons' family rejoice with Steve. The push to victor involves everyone.

Bruce Hazelton

Top Powers' pose says it all.
Bottom The national anthem was never so beautiful or meaningful. (l to r, Marlowe, Dvorak, Saunders, Salmons)

several years earlier, couldn't understand how we got to be so good. He told us he thought we had developed some kind of a movie camera that biochemicially analyzed our opponents as we filmed them. Every time we taped our matches, we were learning something other teams couldn't learn.

He was serious. I couldn't convince him that it wasn't the case. Finally, I told him, "You found us out, Victor. We're using a computer in our cameras. How did you know?"

He was so pleased. I'm certain the Soviets are developing machines just like ours at this very moment.

It reminded me of the movie "Patton," when Patton, played by George C. Scott, was defeating Rommel in the African tank war. "I read your book," Patton kept screaming. We should have been screaming at the Soviets, "We read your book." They had taught us much about volleyball, and now we were throwing it all back at them, with some new twists.

We improved. And when we made the tour in 1984, we had an unbelievable scouting report on the Soviets put together by Crabb. He not only went with us in August of 1983 to the Soviet Union, but scouted the Soviets in the 1983 European Championships in East Germany while the U.S. team played on tour in Japan.

That scouting report made a big difference. We didn't just beat the Soviets, we completely controlled them. At the end of the match, our team was euphoric. We had accomplished something that would be second only to winning the gold medal. I suspected at that match our players knew they were the best.

Then, as we walked back to the locker rooms, I was pulled aside and told the Soviets had just announced a boycott of the Games. It was tough to take. We had just achieved a great victory over a country that has a club program with nearly 100,000 players and total state backing. We were looking forward to the bigger showdown in the Los Angeles Olympics. That's what we wanted; that's what our players wanted; that's what our country wanted. We wanted to beat the best team at the best tournament. Now that would be impossible.

Before I reached our locker room, Platonov came over. He congratulated me, but he was ashen. He said, "We are not going to Los Angeles."

The next day was May 9, a holiday for the Soviets that marked the end of World War II in Europe. Our team and the Soviet team met at a huge memorial and Platonov was in tears. I couldn't figure out if it was because of the boycott or the memory of the war. Then he told me his father had been killed near there in the war. I realized how unimportant volleyball, and the Olympics, really was. The moment put a few things into perspective for me.

It was unclear at that time if the boycott was a threat or a reality. At any rate, I decided not to tell the players the night it was announced. I didn't want to diminish their victory. They had earned it, and telling them the Soviets would not attend the Olympics would put a pall over a big moment in their lives.

The next day at practice, before we went to the memorial, we had to tell our players, and they were crushed. They, too, became distracted. Now two Olympics would be tainted by political machinations. It was disheartening.

Athletes are not usually politically motivated. Whereas countries might not seem to get along, the athletes always seemed to, whether the competition included Soviets or Cubans or our political good friends, the Canadians.

After all, athletes aren't soldiers, and we have something in common with every other athlete in the world. We know how tough it is to be good and what demands are placed on players during practice and training. We don't look upon the Soviet team as a bunch of communists — they're a group of fantastic athletes.

In 1980, our athletes who had trained so hard and qualified for the Olympics, only to be denied, wailed about the opportunity they had lost. It was assumed they were the only unhappy ones. But the teams that did go were unhappy, too. They wanted to perform against the best, and all the best teams were not there.

And we wanted to be the best. We didn't want to win our medals and glory by defeating a lesser group of teams.

That's the way we felt when the Soviets and followers nixed the 1984 Olympics. We felt badly for their teams, who would not be there, and for our team, who would not have the chance to play them.

I must give the Soviet team credit, though. They went through with the rest of the tour, although without winning a game. Their players lost interest and our players lost interest, but at least we were still preparing for the Olympics.

We have respect for the Soviets as sportsmen and human beings. There is no doubt the Soviets had no enthusiasm to play after the boycott was announced, and the Soviet coach had a few discipline problems, too. The first match after the announcement was horrible. Play gradually improved for the other matches, but never did rival the intensity of the first night.

One of their players had said he intended to retire after 1980, but they begged him to stay. After four years of continued training, he had stayed for nothing. Even in the Soviet Union, that can cause a discipline problem.

A lesson that can be learned from something like a boycott. It's a reminder that a team, or individual, shouldn't place all focus on one goal. Sure, the gold medal and play in the Olympics is important, but the goal is the process, not the end result.

When the USA announced the 1980 boycott, our men's volleyball team had not qualified, but the women's team had. They were devastated. They had worked so hard for it, and when the trip was denied, it was tough to recognize the many positive strides made along the way.

Seeing the positive side is easy to say, but not so easy a philosophy to put into practice. All our players ever talked about was the Olympics and the gold medal. Even our coaching staff felt that way. And there was nothing that could be done about it.

There were rumors that the Soviet boycott was just a power play and at the last moment the Soviets would capitulate and show up in Los Angeles, but they never did.

It all made me feel that if countries have such tensions with each other, maybe we shouldn't be competing against each other. On the other hand, if we want to relax those tensions and begin some kind of mutual understanding, maybe playing the Games is the way to do it.

It seemed to me the Soviets could have made a bigger international score by attending the Games rather than boycotting, but it just wasn't going to happen.

A couple of days after the boycott announcement, the Soviet volleyball staff invited our staff to a party. Imagine presidents and generals getting together like that. We had a great time, drinking vodka and eating caviar, fresh meat, and fresh fruit.

We got loose. We went into a sauna to sweat out some of the vodka, came out, and ate some more. Then we went outside to a barbecue, an "American barbecue," they kept calling it. We had lamb sauteed in vodka. They know how to throw a party.

Since we were the only American team in the Soviet Union at the time of the announcement, television crews and other news agencies called on us constantly for exclusive interviews and bugged me more than a little bit. We had just accomplished something grand, winning the first match before the boycott became known, and yet all anyone wanted to talk about was the boycott. Our accomplishment almost went unreported, and didn't seem to mean a thing to those who did report it.

Besides the boycott, the injury to Wilde was also unfortunate. In the last game of the last match, one of the better Soviet players fell under the net, way over on our side. Wilde, trying to block, came down on him and we could tell right away there was a serious injury. He had a double fracture in his lower leg, and it was evident to me he was out of the Olympics. The Soviets took great care of Wilde's leg, but we had to send him home. When the last match was over, we had a dinner with the Soviet team, and Platonov got up and made an emotional speech.

"Do not let this (boycott) affect your enthusiasm for the Olympics," he said. "You have worked hard. I am sorry we can't play."

It was quite an evening.

Next, we went to Czechoslovakia to a small city called Banska Bystricia. It was a relatively strong tournament that included the No. 2 team from the Soviet Union. We cruised. We lost only three games in five matches, and had some of our best passing matches ever. Everyone played great, although for some reason we struggled against the young Soviet team.

I don't know if we felt sorry for them or if they were trying to take out their frustrations on us. Maybe the players were just trying to show they should be on the No. 1 team.

ABC television interviewed us about the boycott, not about how well we had been playing. I suppose I wouldn't have been so angry if someone had paid at least a little attention to us before, but no one had. Now we had to do the explaining for the Soviets. I hated that.

We did have one incident with a Czech reporter. He understood English and had a tape recorder.

The Soviets said that two reasons for their boycott were the lack of security for the athletes and the crass commercialization of the games by Los Angeles.

"Mr. Beal, I want to be very clear about this," the reporter said. "Please be honest in your response. Do you think the Los Angeles committee has gone to excess on commercializing the Games?"

"They've done some good things, but there are some things I don't like," I answered while my interpreter cringed. "In general, it's been great. There are no security problems. We want to protect the Soviet Union's athletes and all athletes."

Neville looked at me with his you've-done-it-again look.

The next day the papers came out and our interpreter was ready to sue.

"You see this headline," he says. "It reads: 'American coach endorses Soviet boycott.' I don't know how that guy could have gotten that out of what you said, but it would have been better had you not said anything." I don't have very good luck with reporters.

The way we figured it, we were the best team in the world, even if the Soviets and Cubans had attended the Olympics. At the same time, I didn't think we should be favored in the Olympics because we really hadn't proven our standing in international competition at the major tournaments. This may sound like double talk, but there is a difference between feeling like the best and proving you're the best. As a coaching staff and as a team, we felt we could beat anybody at any time. All we needed now was the forum of the Olympics to prove it.

Only the Soviets, Cuba, and Brazil could compete with us internationally. When we got back to San Diego, we felt like our success had been noticed. The people accepted us warmly and held a banquet in our honor. We appreciated it.

Ten days later, we had to go on our annual tour of Japan.

Marlowe was back with us and it was interesting to see how the team reacted. The team had begun to accept Wilde for his playing, and they missed him. They had developed a respect for Wilde, which was positive feedback.

In Japan, we played well, subbing a lot and then playing our best team in the final match, which proved to be our best showing.

Back home, we took a 10-day break and then China's team came over. The Chinese were not equal competition, and we won all three matches 3-0. At the end of that tour, we cut Blanchard.

What a tough cut to make. Blanchard was the hardest-working player we had. He never missed a competition or practice. He never argued. We simply didn't have a position for him. We didn't have a role for him to play. By this time, we couldn't be concerned with who deserved to play. We wanted to have our best team for the Olympics. And the feelings of a player who wasn't going to make the team had to be set aside. It's the worst part of coaching, but it has to be done.

Little time was left, but we continued playing matches to stay sharp. We staged a USA Cup Tournament in San Diego in front of some strangely paltry crowds. Maybe people were used to us winning too much or perhaps the Olympics were just too close, but the tournament didn't draw well. It was also summer, and the San Diego Padres were involved in winning their first division championship and pennant in the history of the franchise. I guess people wanted to save their money for the Olympics. Tickets certainly weren't cheap.

We wanted one team from our pool in the Olympics to play, and Argentina came over. China stayed and we tried to get another team, but couldn't. We used a college all-star squad.

We didn't lose a game, and after the tournament we went up to San Francisco to play Argentina one more time on June 27. We won, 3-0, although the final game was 17-15.

It was our last match before the Olympics, and we had won 25 straight. For the year, we were 34-9 and 18-5 at home.

We were prepared and anxious. For our final training, we didn't want to stay in San Diego, where the media would find us, and family and friends would bug us. We wanted peace and quiet. We looked around for a suitable place to go, and found it in Pullman, Washington.

Chapter 14.

Alone in Washington State: Getting ready.

The Olympics were just a few weeks away and it was time to steel ourselves for the biggest matches of our lives. There were so many distractions in San Diego, we felt we had to find another site to gather ourselves together. We wanted something very much like Outward Bound, only not quite as emotional and without the same hardships.

We also wanted to prepare our team in a large arena that would simulate the Long Beach Arena, and we needed to stay in the same time zone. The environment had to be conducive to the final push.

To our staff, this was the logical thing to do. To the players, it was less than logical. They didn't want to leave San Diego again.

Here we were, moving the team again, and not all the players were happy about it. But there was much less grumbling about this move than for the Outward Bound preparation. This was more acceptable. There would be no 70-pound packs to carry, and everyone would have a bed, not to mention toilet paper.

Over the years, we always had this conflict with the team, which I suppose happens with all teams in different ways. The players feel you should have them only for their time on the floor or on the field. Management always feels the players are theirs at all hours, all times.

The players wanted to be alone in San Diego. We wanted them to be alone, together, in Pullman, Washington. After the team took a few days off, we went.

Tony Crabb found the site for us. Pullman is a quiet town and would give us some attention without being overbearing.

Jim Coleman was the coach at Washington State, so that gave us somebody we knew well on site. Since we had our schedule for the Olympics, we tried to match it up with this final preparation as best we could. We didn't figure we were going to lose at the Olympics, so we played some scrimmages on that basis.

The arena on the Washington State campus was large and the people in town accepted us graciously. We had some incredible crowds there. Most of our scrimmages were virtually unannounced, yet thousands of people came out to watch, and one ghost came back to haunt me.

An NBC news crew came in to film us and talk about the team for the Nightly News.

The first thing the reporter said to me was, "Mike Dodd called you a fascist dictator. What do you say to that?"

First of all, I didn't think Dodd knew what a fascist was. Dodd's the guy who was ruled ineligible for the NORCECA games in Mexico. We let him stay with us the rest of the year anyway, while we were appealing his case so he could become an amateur again. Since he couldn't participate with us at that time, he asked if he could go to Italy, make some money, and return in May.

That was all right with us because he would be concentrating on volleyball. Finally, his amateur papers came through after a lot of work by our staff, and Dodd said, "Sorry, I don't want to play on your team." Then he called me a fascist.

In Italy, he had become great friends with Hovland.

Well, I'm not a fascist, but I am a dictator. I'm in charge of the program. We don't vote here. I'm happy to be called a dictator. In the 1976 Olympics, after the U.S. basketball team lost a controversial game to the Soviet Union in the final, they refused to accept the silver medal. Maryland basketball Coach Lefty Driesell told U.S. Coach Hank Iba his team should have accepted the silver medal anyway.

"But the team voted not to accept the medal," Iba said.

"My players often take votes," Driesell said. "But *I* am the head coach."

At our Washington hideaway, we followed the Olympic schedule. When the schedule said we were to play a match, we divided the squad and played, inviting the public to watch. We not only played on our Olympic schedule, we ate on it, too.

There were a few things we did we hoped we wouldn't do at the Olympics. We had some horrible practices and in our last scrimmage, we almost had a fight.

The team was on edge. I was edgy myself. When I look back, I suspect I pushed the guys a bit too hard. We had taken two referees with us and told them to call the play tougher than it would be called in the actual Games. Every drill and scrimmage was officiated, tightly and harshly, and most drills were run as competitions, all of which heightened the tension. The whole ordeal built to a head on the final night in the fifth game of the match.

I coached one team and Neville and Crabb had the other. I had Dvorak, the other team had Marlowe. At one point, there was a disputed call against my team. Marlowe, a feisty guy, said something that made the situation worse.

Timmons and Powers half started across the net and some players had to pull them back. Then Dvorak said a few things to Marlowe, and when it was over, the majority of players wouldn't even shake hands.

At the Olympics, we never lost control. When we lost that match to Brazil, we didn't point fingers. Everything came together just as it should have.

The rest of the time in Pullman was spent going over scouting reports and watching videos of the other teams. The near fight was forgotten once the Games began.

We had quality time in Pullman. The people treated us spectacularly. They hosted us at dinners. They watched our matches.

Then, it was time to go. On July 22, we flew directly to Los Angeles.

Chapter 15.

The Olympic Games.

The saying is, "There are a lot of upsets in the morning."

Olympic scheduling isn't a simple matter — who you play, when you play, and when you don't are critical considerations.

Earlier in the summer, we received a copy of our schedule, and as the host team, we had some advantages at the draw, which was held in Barcelona, Spain.

Hosts are allowed three choices: 1) to pick the team they want to open against, 2) to pick when to play one other team, and 3) to choose when they want their day off during the tournament.

At the site of the draw, a big chart called the Berger Table is used for the selection process. Once the host team makes their three choices, everything else falls into place on the Berger Table, and the rest of the tournament is drawn up.

We naturally wanted to set up the tournament to our advantage, so we gave serious thought to the procedure.

The tournament would have ten teams, and after pool round-robin play, there would be a crossover involving the top two teams advancing to the medal round. Originally, before the boycott, our pool had Brazil, Bulgaria, Poland, and Argentina as well as us. The other pool was made up of Japan, Egypt, Cuba, Canada, and the Soviet Union.

We thought Brazil was the best competition in our pool and kicked around whether we should play them first or last. We decided to wait to play Brazil and open with Argentina. Not the best team in the pool, but not the worst, either, Argentina tended to improve as they advanced in tournaments. We figured that if they were going to get better, we didn't want them to get better against us. We decided to get Argentina out of the way as soon as possible.

Then, we decided to take one of our days off right before the match with

133

Brazil. It was planned that Brazil would have its toughest match against Poland just before they played us. But it turned out to be Korea, an addition to the tourney after the boycott was announced.

Even though it had not made the original field, Korea was a good team, something the Brazilians apparently overlooked.

It was also important for us to play on a regular schedule. Matches were set up in pairs, two in the daytime and two in the evening. The early matches were at 10 and noon; the evening matches at 6:30 and 8:30. We weren't inclined to play in the morning and were tempted to go with the 6:30 p.m. time slot so we'd know exactly when our matches would begin and not have to wait if a previous match ran long.

However, ABC television told us we'd have a better chance of getting on the air if we played the later match. We went along with that. It took about five seconds for us to decide in ABC's favor. And we did get good coverage on television, for the first time ever.

Morning matches are horrible, which means the matches in Korea for the 1988 Games will be brutal. We'll have to think of something there. Television, again, wants to broadcast live, and to get live TV back to the United States from Korea means morning matches. In 1977, at the World University Games in Bulgaria, we had to play two morning matches, against Italy and Yugoslavia. We lost. To play an 8 a.m. match we had to get up at 5. There *are* a lot of upsets in the morning.

Training during the Olympics was a concern because of logistics. There were two Olympic Villages, one on the UCLA campus and one on the USC campus. The American athletes stayed at USC, but that was a long way from Long Beach Arena, possibly 45 minutes. We wanted to make sure we had time to practice, eat well, and give our players time to enjoy the rest of the games with their families and friends.

That's an important part of the Olympics. Athletes should be allowed to meet each other — not only those in their own sport, but in the other sports, too.

Because of the distance between sites, we secured hotel rooms near the arena, and after games the players stayed there. Nights before matches, we stayed at the Olympic Village. It cost us a lot of money to do that, but that's one of the elements in sports that allows a team to be successful — a good budget. There was no sense running our team around town day after day and then expecting peak performances during the matches. We wanted to make certain we had at least some rest.

On the day we arrived in Los Angeles, we stayed at the Airport Marriott, which is where the teams lined up to get their Olympic gear. We call it "booty day," and sometimes I think the athletes live for this day more than any other. This is where clothing and equipment are handed out, and it's quite a harvest.

Levi's was outfitting the American teams, and we received all sorts of goods, from the uniforms we wore marching into opening ceremonies to the sweat pants we were supposed to wear on the victory stands.

One of the great things about international competition is the trading of clothes and other goods among athletes.

At the 1973 World University Games in the Soviet Union, Marlowe was known as King of the Traders. He went over there with an extra suitcase filled with nothing but sweatsuits and jeans and all kinds of American goods. On the last day, he went around to other athletes' rooms and began trading. He got a beautiful African robe and a bunch of other souvenirs. Guys were right behind him trading for the things he had just traded.

Anyway, that's also part of the Games.

We thought we were going to be able to hold a practice later on that day, but by the time we arrived at the Village, we were running so late, we canceled. That made it two straight days without any training, which was a concern, but we had to live with that as I'm sure the other teams did, too.

Before we entered the USC village, I tried to make my team aware of security problems. I told everyone not to wear any USA clothing outside the gates, advice, of course, that was largely ignored. I also told them to be wary of two types of terrorists — foreigners wearing fatigues or turbans and carrying semi-automatic weapons, and disgruntled beach volleyball players wearing trunks, shades, and moneybelts, and carrying umbrella poles.

I made it very clear I was more concerned about the latter group.

The village had everything from free movies for the athletes to free concerts, video games, and food. Banks and the 7-11 store were not free. Haircuts were, and Vidal Sassoon was on hand. Timmons and Kiraly got their hair styled sort of punk. It was an attention grabber, all right. Marlowe got his hair styled too, and wondered why I didn't go for it. I said those guys doing the hair weren't going to touch mine. There were lots of things I was willing to do for the Olympics; that wasn't one of them.

On July 24, we finally held our first practice in the Long Beach Arena, one of the two days we were allowed to practice on the Games site. I was excited just walking in there. It was quite a thrill. I got there early and watched one of the other teams practice and when I saw how the place was decorated, I realized the committee in charge of volleyball had done an outstanding job.

The Long Beach Arena is not an ideal arena for volleyball. The stands are far away and I had always felt the place had a cold feeling. Not now. It was beautiful. No national colors were used at any of the venues, but a lot of pastels were in evidence. The committee had created a great feeling. I enjoyed every moment I spent in that arena. I had a real tingling feeling.

While the other team practiced, I must have walked around and sat in 100 different seats. I walked into all the locker rooms and the medical rooms and the offices. I wanted to see everything.

When it came time for our practice, there was some discussion as to whether we wanted to clear the arena or allow people to wander in and out as we had done. We did try to clear some people out, but it didn't do any good. There must have been 2,000 workers around, so we just forgot about it and practiced.

It was a horrible practice, at least by my standards. I'm rarely happy with practice, but this one was especially bad. Crabb told me not to worry. We hadn't played anyone in a while, and the guys were a little tight.

Our other practices were held at facilities near the USC campus. We tried to arrange a scrimmage with one of the other teams in the Olympics, but had some trouble. Nobody wanted to practice against a team it might have to play. Finally, we matched up with China at our final practice in the Long Beach Arena. We didn't keep score, but we didn't play very well. I had some apprehension about that. It was evident to me the team was tight, and I didn't want it to stay that way.

The night before the Opening Ceremonies, the 27th we had a dinner for team members only. It was there McPeak passed out special gold medal watches that Crabb had arranged for all the players and staff to receive from the USVBA. That was a nice touch, and it brought everyone involved with the long struggle a little closer together.

Sleep was difficult that night. I had as much anticipation for the Opening Ceremonies as I did the opening matches.

For the ceremonies, we didn't just walk in. Everyone had to gather at the nearby Sports Arena and wait turns. We were in there three hours before our time came, but what we saw would have been worth another three-hour wait.

As nervous as we were about our opening match, the Opening Ceremonies took our minds off it. Some pressure was released. Everyone pressed in close together, not only the volleyball team, but all the teams. We were also teammates with the American basketball players, and the track athletes, and the swimmers. It was quite a feeling.

It was also great to be able to share those moments with friends. Neville and Crabb and I walked into that Coliseum together and had a magnificent time. It was fun and beautiful. There are few events today that can match such splendor.

We really enjoyed the Olympics. It was an overwhelming experience to see Rafer Johnson carry that torch to the top of the stadium. It set the tone of the entire event. For the team, the sense of that event set the tone of the entire Games.

Finally, on the next night, July 29, we played our first match, against Argentina.

Tunisia had been added to our pool along with Korea, taking the places of Poland and Bulgaria. Tunisia was obviously the weakest team, but we were happy with our draw against Argentina. In the morning we practiced, then bused to the hotel near the arena. The team rested and had its prematch meal. It was Dvorak's 26th birthday.

He got a nice present that night. We won.

I was happy to be playing a match finally — we were the first U.S. team to play — and I played everybody. We wanted all our players to have an Olympic experience right off the bat, and if we lost a game in the process, that was all right. Even if we had to go to five games against Argentina, we felt comfortable we'd win with no problems.

The match went four games, with Argentina winning the third. The scores were 15-6, 15-7, 10-15, 15-8. Powers struggled a bit, having trouble with his approach rhythm, so we pulled him. Later in the tournament he came back to be awesome. Timmons was overwhelmed emotionally, and Kiraly was screaming and got a little carried away at some of the other players' mistakes.

This was the Olympics, and emotions were high. It was an intense time.

Our next match was with Tunisia, a weak team, but we weren't going to make a big deal out of their weakness. We couldn't afford to plant the seed that the match would be easy and have our guys go in at marginal intensity. There's nothing worse than going into a match or a game thinking a big effort won't be needed, and then losing.

We decided to play Salmons instead of Buck for this match, and it turned out to be hardly a warmup. We beat Tunisia 15-3, 15-2, 15-3 on July 31 and I don't know how they got eight points.

Korea was to be our third match, and it was a key one for us. Although Korea eventually finished fifth in the tournament, it lost only one match, to us. That's because only two teams from each pool could advance to the medal round. If teams are tied for matches won, the tiebreaker is games won. Korea went on to beat Brazil and Brazil beat us. Had we beaten Brazil, Korea would have advanced to the medal round, not Brazil.

That's why the Koreans were so upset with us for not beating Brazil in the round robin.

Korea was a very good team, but we beat them, 15-13, 15-9, 15-6. We didn't yet have our best team on the floor. We still weren't using Powers and Buck as much as we would be — we wanted to ease them into the Olympic atmosphere — and they were keys to our team.

Korea's fifth place finish was the highest they could go once they failed to reach the medal round. It was the same sort of situation we faced in the World Championships. Even though we might have been better than other teams advancing from the other pools, we still could finish no better than 13th. Now Korea, probably the third best team in the Olympics, could only finish fifth. That might not seem to be much of a difference, but it's the difference between nothing and a bronze medal at the Games.

On our day off, we watched Korea beat Brazil, and that changed our feeling about our Brazil match. We were in the semis now, and didn't have to win to be there. We didn't even have to win a game to get into the medal round. Also, we knew Brazil would have to play a better match against us to reach the medal round.

The match took place on August 6. We kept Sunderland and Salmons in the starting lineup, and as the match progressed, we used everybody on the bench. But nothing we did could change the tenor of the match. Brazil played great; we played poorly. Kiraly hit minus 23 percent, his single worst percentage in four years. We had problems receiving their power serve and purposely made no effort to block it, a change we had made for the gold medal match. We did put Powers back into the lineup in the middle of that first match with Brazil, and he was spectacular in the rest of the Games.

We were certain we'd be facing Brazil for the gold medal because our semi was against Canada and Brazil's was against Italy, another last-minute replacement team. We knew what changes we wanted to make for the Brazil match and best of all, our practices began to sharpen up. The guys were focusing a little more.

We beat Canada quite easily, 15-6, 15-10, 15-7, although they did get ahead in each game. We passed fantastically well, but we didn't block very well. We never got aced, which is amazing. Kiraly and Berzins passed almost perfectly and just about everyone played a fantastic match. None of the games even went five full rotations.

We had made the gold medal match. We were confident. We had recovered our rhythm. We thought if we got on top of Brazil, we'd blow them away.

Our last practice was a tough one, and again the team thought we pushed too hard (why change a successful pattern), but we didn't want to lose our competitive edge. There was a lot of tension at that practice, but it was a good one.

After the morning practice on August 11, we went to the Long Beach Arena and saw parents and friends. Neville, Crabb, and I usually had a meeting on match day, but this one lasted only about three minutes. The reports were all over my bed. We looked at each other and laughed. There really wasn't anything more to talk about.

We had a cookbook of what we wanted done. I read once that Bill Walsh of the 49ers wrote out all the plays he wanted to start a game. We couldn't do that exactly because our game is continuous motion, but we came close to Walsh's idea.

We had our rotation down. We had our setting tendencies down, our passing down. Our matchups were perfect.

We made one key change that worked well. We changed Berzins' blocking assignment. In our first match with Brazil, Aldis had no stuffs and the team only nine. In the gold medal match, he had four stuffs, the team had 13. Berzins set the tempo in the first game with three stuffs.

Brazil got only 19 points. In the first two games of our first match with them, we had 92 rotations and 115 for the entire match, but this match took only 73 rotations. We handled their spike serve by putting a blocker in front of it. We had an attack efficiency of almost 50 percent. We had a 60 percent kill ratio. Buck made no hitting errors and was an intimidator. Timmons was great from the back row. Powers and Timmons had carried us in our final two matches and couldn't have been any better, especially offensively.

There were so many things that happened that night. I didn't watch the bronze medal match but hoped that Canada would win so North America could have two medals. Lamentably, Canada played an uninspired match against Italy and lost 3-0. The crowd cleared out and I went to the arena early, already dressed for the match, and sat awhile in the empty stands with Neville. We absorbed the moment and tried to make it last as long as we could.

The players finally arrived and I sent them to the warmup court with Bill. He's really offended when people think of him as only a motivator, because that's just part of what he does. He does a great deal very well and happens to be fantastic at relating to players. I don't know what he said in warmups, but it must have been just right. The guys were certainly ready. In that situation, a team could hardly not be.

I kept walking from our locker room through the tunnel to look in the arena where the crowd was filing in. I recognized so many faces. And then the team came into the locker room for final instructions, and Tom Selleck came in to say a few words.

Security was tight and we only had a few moments before the lineup for introductions. Selleck had his say and left.

Then I said a few words. Whether anyone paid attention, I don't know, but at least they did a good job faking it. All eyes were on me. Before we knew it, the players were out in the hallway. They were introduced and went into their final warmup.

The match went by much too quickly. I enjoyed every minute of it. I enjoyed the time outs. I enjoyed the time between games. It was one of the most unbelievable times of my life.

A play in the first game set the tone. We were well ahead, but out of position when a Brazilian spiked the ball for an apparent point. Yet even as the Brazilians were celebrating, the ball hit Buck on the shoulder and bounced straight up. Dvorak set it and Timmons killed it for side out. It was a stunning play, and served notice that we would do little wrong.

I called no time outs in the first game and one each in the second and third. In the second game, Brazil had taken a 5-2 lead when I called time earlier than normal to stop their momentum.

Brazil scored only one more point that game, and we took a 2-0 game lead.

The place was a madhouse. As much as the Olympic committee tried to keep the Olympics nonnational, this was our home, and some American touches were added to the festivities.

"Let's Hear It For The Boy(s)" kept blaring over the loud speaker, and the crowd was in a frenzy. Keeping still on the bench was an absolute chore.

Mr. Chin, from China, was the referee, the same referee we had for the first Brazil match. I was happy about that. In fact, I thought the officiating was good throughout the tournament. I had been worried because the boycotting countries had no officials there, and they tended to be the best officials in the world.

The final score was 15-6, 15-6, 15-7. Brazil had 73 opportunities to score but scored on only 13 rotations. Our defense was awesome, our offense as smooth as it has ever been. It was a great night for volleyball in the United States.

I saw Glen Davies, a retired referee and USVBA official. He had refereed the gold medal match in the 1976 Games, a high honor. He was one of our greatest supporters, and had even gone on a trip with us in early June. I found him before the medal ceremony and rushed into his arms after the victory.

I tried to find McPeak. He was such a driving force.

Many times over the years McPeak and I had discussed shortcuts to making the team better, but he always looked at the long run. He was our conscience. I saw him in the runway. Oh, man, was he happy.

We were going crazy internally before the last point and here we were, just a few feet away from some of the greats of the game. Matsudaira of Japan was sitting behind us, and Chesnekov of the Soviet Union. They had taught us so much.

The last point developed into a one-on-one confrontation. It was Brazil's best attacker, Rajman, against Dvorak. Rajman tried to go down the line, but Dusty made a great solo stuff block.

And it was over.

Chapter 16.

Aftermath.

Timmons leaped onto the referee's stand, and other guys were in various stages of celebration. Marlowe carried a huge American flag around the floor.

I coaxed Wilde and Blanchard to come out of the stands and join us, too. We included them in our special Olympics edition program because of the large part they played along the way to our gold medal.

Then the house lights went down and the trumpets blared and the medals came out and the National Anthem played. I try not to show my emotions and am usually not an emotional guy, but this was too much.

Later, we had a fabulous party back at the hotel. I still hadn't found my parents, but spotted them across the huge lobby at the Hyatt Hotel. I was soaked from perspiration, so I decided to go up to my room first and change. I did that quickly.

When I came down, my father was waiting for me as I got off the elevator.

This was a guy who always wanted to know what his kid was getting into from the time he was just in junior high. Dad had a lot of meetings with my coaches about why I was out so late and why I went to so many competitions and spent so much time reading books on volleyball. Those coaches told him I was just learning the game of volleyball.

We had a nice quiet talk in front of those elevators on the way to the party, funded by the USVBA, Don Sammis, and my dad. He had one of those Olympic coin sets in his hand. He knew coaches didn't get gold medals, only players. One of the coins in the set was gold. He handed the set over to me.

"I think you deserve a gold medal, too," he said. It was another special moment.

* * *

We had made great strides over the years, but there are many more strides

141

to make. We must ensure that our 1984 victory wasn't a bolt of lightning in the dark. We must continue to be successful, although we won't be failures by any means if we don't win the gold medal every four years. We must try to do our best.

If we do that, we will win, again and again.

I had decided I wouldn't seek the coaching position again just after we got back from Europe in May of 1984. But I will be staying with the program in a new capacity, as National Team Director, with Tony Crabb as my asistant. The job is new, much like that of an athletic director at a large university.

Before, we were fragmented and duties were passed among a number of people. Now, we'll have a level of continuity in the entire elite volleyball community.

The men's and women's teams will train in San Diego. The Junior National teams, the World University Games teams, our teams for the National Sports Festival and the youth development teams will train at various times in Colorado Springs. I will direct their programs, too.

It gives us a special sense of pride to have the women's team training under the same framework as our men's program. It underlines our program's success and acceptance. The feeling that the women's team was ignored after the Olympics has caused some bitterness and backlash, a feeling we hope to remedy.

Marv Dunphy, the highly successful coach at Pepperdine, became the new National men's coach a month or so after the Olympics, and he will be a good one.

Dunphy will also be more popular with the players. He's a player's coach, and spends more time relating to the team. He can take our team in a new direction. They need a change, and this one is very positive.

Taras Liskevych, from the University of the Pacific, is the new women's coach. His extensive background makes him a wise choice. Liskevych followed me as coach at Ohio State. He and Marv get along well, which will be important with both teams being in the same city. They can share ideas on training and strategy.

Neville went back to Montana State University in Bozeman to be head women's coach there, and Crabb coached the men's team just after the Olympics until Dunphy took over.

We will continue our search for sponsors. Business support tends to slack off between Olympic years. However, some of our sponsors have stayed with us, and the Los Angeles Olympic Committee has given us $1,300,000. Sounds like a lot, but it will be quickly used for our expanding program.

Our women's team members will be looking for jobs for the first time, and we're hoping that because of the success of both teams in LA, more jobs will become available.

Klostermann is staying on as head of the jobs program, and director of the San Diego office.

We also have an arrangement with IMG, a sports marketing agency out of Cleveland and New York. IMG has put together several tours for us with television coverage. They feel our men's team is marketable, as long as it retains at least some of the Olympic players — and eight have continued on with the team after the Games. We hope to find an effective way to market our women's team as well.

The only bad news after our victory in Los Angeles was a knee injury suffered by Timmons on the trip to Korea. I hope it heals because he has such a bright future in the sport. Of the eight players who stayed with the team, probably four or five will still be with the team in Seoul during the 1988 Games.

This is a new era for amateur sports. Some of the old attitudes are changing and amateur athletics is taking on a new look. There is money involved now, for teams, and for individuals. Some may argue this is not true amateurism. Actually, it's a realistic approach that allows athletes the freedom to train and prepare for international competition. The Olympics clearly demonstrated the special feeling that exists for amateur athletics.

Changes are happening so quickly I often think of that scene in the movie "2001" when the lights come at you from all directions and you get a tremendous sensation of passing time, distance, worlds, and eons. All the principles and constructs people were used to have changed.

In volleyball, we lead the way in professional staffing, corporate fundraising, and dealing with our athletes.

Where will it all lead? Some day, we won't need a program like this. There will be as many volleyball players out there as basketball players, and teams will be put together in a summer and be able to compete. We'll be able to perpetuate the sport without a national training center.

We have some name recognition now, for the first time. Not only among the men, but with Rita Crockett, Debbie Green, and Flo Hyman of the women's team, too.

I also hear rumors of a new pro league, which, if it happens, will serve to advertise the sport.

So much has happened. Snow, Dayton, Wright State, Roosevelt Center, defeat, victory, despair, Jim Coleman, revival, San Diego, Sammis, Outward Bound, Selleck, the Soviet Union, boycott, perspective, tactics, victory, Blanchard, Wilde, Washington State, Olympics, Opening Ceremony, Neville, Crabb, Argentina, Tunisia, Korea, Brazil, Canada, Saunders, Sunderland, Powers, Kiraly, Salmons, Waldie, Timmons, Buck, Berzins, Duwelius, Marlowe, Brazil, Dvorak, victory, gold.

We have just taken the first step in a great growth period. And we have made history.

USA Team '81-'84 Results

1981 RESULTS

USA VS. BRAZIL:
(June 3-14)
BRAZIL 3, USA 1 (15-12, 12-15, 15-6, 15-13) @ San Diego, CA.
USA 3, BRAZIL 0 (15-9, 15-10, 15-11) @ Huntington Beach, CA.
USA 3, BRAZIL 2 (15-12, 14-16, 15-13, 12-15, 15-12) @ Santa Barbara, CA.
USA 3, BRAZIL 0 (15-10, 15-12, 15-8) @ San Luis Obispo, CA.
USA 3, BRAZIL 1 (16-14, 15-11, 14-16, 15-8) @ Bakersfield, CA.
BRAZIL 3, USA 1 (15-5, 15-12, 12-15, 15-10) @ Fresno, CA.
BRAZIL 3, USA 1 (18-16, 15-9, 9-15, 15-9) @ Sacramento, CA.
USA 3, BRAZIL 1 (15-12, 14-16, 15-3, 15-5) @ Berkeley, CA.
BRAZIL 3, USA 1 (6-15, 15-8, 15-6, 16-14) @ San Jose, CA.

"We began the quadrennial with a close 5-4 match win over Brazil. Who was to know that we would end our Olypmic quest with this same opponent. Things do come full circle."

USA VS. CANADA:
(June 27)
USA 3, CANADA 0 (15-8, 15-7, 15-8) @ San Diego, CA.

NORCECA ZONE CHAMPIONSHIPS: MEXICO CITY
(July 4-9)
USA 3, GUATEMALA 0 (15-3, 15-2, 15-5)
USA 3, DOMINICAN REPUBLIC 0 (15-4, 15-7, 15-5)
USA 3, PANAMA 0 (15-3, 15-6, 15-0)
USA 3, MEXICO 0 (15-9, 15-8, 15-5)
USA 3, CANADA 2 (8-15, 15-12, 8-15, 15-12, 15-8)
CUBA 3, USA 2 (12-15, 16-14, 15-10, 5-15, 15-13)

"A very tough loss in the finals to Cuba. I learned a great deal about the team under pressure in this tournament. Our flexible system won in the semi's against Canada."

TOUR OF JAPAN:
(July 26-August 2)
JAPAN 3, USA 2 (15-12, 8-15, 15-4, 11-15, 15-6) @ Tokyo
JAPAN 3, USA 2 (14-16, 13-15, 15-7, 15-8, 16-14) @ Saku
JAPAN 3, USA 0 (15-11, 15-11, 15-12) @ Tatsuno
JAPAN 3, USA 2 (19-17, 15-7, 5-15, 16-18, 15-13) @ Nagoya
JAPAN 3, USA 2 (15-10, 15-8, 13-15, 6-15, 15-13) @ Osaka

"Japan was not easy to overcome, especially at home. In the second match we had a 14-4 lead in game #5! Somehow we lost 3 matches after being at deuce in the 5th game!"

1981 FRIENDSHIP CUP COMPETITION VS. JAPAN:
(August 6-9)
USA 3, JAPAN 2 (11-15, 10-15, 15-13, 15-9, 15-7) @ San Diego, CA

JAPAN 3, USA 2 (17-15, 10-15, 6-15, 15-12, 15-9) @ Tucson, AZ.
USA 3, JAPAN 0 (16-14, 15-6, 15-12) @ Phoenix, AZ.
USA 3, JAPAN 1 (6-15, 17-15, 15-11, 15-4) @ Denver, CO.

"We beat Japan's National Team for the first time since 1969!"

USA VS. CANADA:
(October 21-24)
USA 3, CANADA 1 (15-9, 15-7, 8-15, 15-5) @ Cheney, WA.
USA 3, CANADA 0 (15-9, 15-6, 15-12) @ Walla Walla, WA.
USA 3, CANADA 1 (12-15, 15-7, 15-11, 15-13) @ Boise, ID.

USA VS. BRAZIL:
(November 3-4)
BRAZIL 3, USA 2 (16-14, 15-9, 10-15, 12-15, 15-13) @ Los Angeles, CA.
USA 3, BRAZIL 2 (13-15, 11-15, 15-4, 15-8, 16-14) @ San Diego, CA.

"It's still close with Brazil!"

CANADA CUP TOURNAMENT — WINNIPEG, MANITOBA:
(November 8-12)
USA 3, CANADA 0 (15-13, 15-11, 15-10)
CUBA 3, USA 2 (15-3, 5-15, 5-15, 15-10, 15-11)
USA 3, BRAZIL 0 (15-13, 15-12, 15-7)
USA 3, CANADA 0 (15-6, 15-6, 15-10)
USA 3, CUBA 1 (15-13, 8-15, 15-12, 15-6)

"Our first big tournament win, and our first win over Cuba since 1973!!"

1981 OVERALL RECORD: 22-13
RECORD IN U.S.: 13-6

1982 RESULTS

USA VS. CANADA:
(March 1-7)
USA 3, CANADA 0 (15-12, 15-7, 15-8) @ Bellingham, WA.
USA 3, CANADA 2 (19-17, 15-5, 12-15, 12-15, 15-13) @ Yakima, WA.
USA 3, CANADA 0 (15-5, 15-9, 15-5) @ Corvallis, OR.
USA 3, CANADA 2 (12-15, 15-5, 8-15, 15-13, 15-10) @ Portland, OR.
USA 3, CANADA 2 (15-8, 12-15, 15-11, 13-15, 15-10) @ Tumwater, WA.

"Canada just can't buy a win over the USA!"

USA VS. MEXICO:
(June 18-19)
USA 3, MEXICO 0 (15-2, 15-5, 15-12) @ Long Beach, CA.
USA 3, MEXICO 1 (15-7, 7-15, 15-3, 15-3) @ San Diego, CA.

SHANGHAI INVITATIONAL TOURNAMENT: SHANGHAI, CHINA
(June 25-July 7)
USA 3, YUGOSLAVIA 1 (15-4, 12-15, 15-8, 15-13)
USA 3, FRANCE 1 (15-10, 11-15, 15-2, 15-3)
USA 3, CHINA YOUTH NATIONAL 2 (8-15, 10-15, 15-9, 15-8, 15-11)
CHINA 3, USA 2 (14-16, 12-15, 15-11, 16-14, 15-6)
BRAZIL 3, USA 2 (6-15, 14-16, 15-10, 15-5, 15-12)

USA 3, JAPAN 1 (15-10, 7-15, 15-8, 15-4)
USA 3, SHANGHAI CLUB 2 (15-7, 11-15, 11-15, 15-10, 15-6)
USA 3, JIANGSU CLUB 0 (15-5, 15-8, 16-14)
CHINA 3, USA 2 (15-8, 13-15, 2-15, 15-11, 15-12)

"China played great at home to win 2 very long 5-game matches. Brazil beat us by slowing the match down with delays and complaints. We lost our concentration — finished 3rd in Shanghai!"

SEOUL INTERNATIONAL GOODWILL
MEN'S VOLLEYBALL TOURNAMENT: SEOUL, KOREA
(July 13-20)
USA 3, KOREA 0 (15-4, 16-14, 18-16)
USA 3, INDIA 0 (15-4, 15-4, 15-12)
USA 3, CANADA 0 (15-7, 15-5, 15-5)
USA 3, KOREA 0 (15-6, 15-10, 15-13)
USA 3, SOGANG UNIVERSITY 0 (15-6, 16-14, 15-1)
USA 3, IN-HA UNIVERSITY 0 (15-3, 15-7, 15-7)

"An easy tournament win in the middle of a very long Orient trip."

TOUR OF JAPAN:
(July 24-August 1)
JAPAN 3, USA 0 (15-9, 15-12, 15-9) @ Hirosaki
USA 3, JAPAN 2 (3-15, 15-9, 14-16, 15-5, 15-11) @ Nakamitta
USA 3, JAPAN 0 (15-10, 15-8, 19-17) @ Hakodate
JAPAN 3, USA 0 (15-12, 15-9, 15-9) @ Imawazawa
JAPAN 3, USA 2 (13-15, 15-9, 15-11, 10-15, 15-11) @ Tomakomai
USA 3, JAPAN 1 (12-15, 15-6, 15-2, 15-3) @ Tokyo
JAPAN 3, USA 1 (15-13, 15-9, 8-15, 15-9) @ Nagoya

"We win our first ever matches in Japan. Over these seven matches and 27 games the Japanese score 7 more points than we do — right now we are better than Japan!"

USA VS ITALY:
(August 7-12)
USA 3, ITALY 0 (15-11, 15-13, 15-13) @ Waukegan, IL.
USA 3, ITALY 1 (15-12, 13-15, 15-11, 15-8) @ Chicago, IL.
ITALY 3, USA 0 (15-11, 15-7, 15-9) @ Grand Rapids, MI.
USA 3, ITALY 0 (15-5, 15-5, 15-11) @ Denver, CO.
ITALY 3, USA 0 (15-9, 15-8, 15-13) @ Colorado Springs, CO.

USA VS. KOREA:
(September 7-12)
USA 3, KOREA 0 (15-11, 15-8, 15-8) @ San Diego, CA.
USA 3, KOREA 1 (12-15, 15-5, 17-15, 15-12) @ Fresno, CA.
USA 3, KOREA 1 (15-5, 5-15, 15-3, 15-12) @ Los Angeles, CA.
KOREA 3, USA 0 (15-8, 15-9, 15-10) @ Berkeley, CA.
USA 3, KOREA 0 (15-12, 15-3, 15-1) @ Sacramento, CA.

"We crush Korea as we begin to prepare and hone down for the World Championships. (Korea finishes 8th at World Championships; we are 6-1 against Korea)"

USA VS. POLAND:
(September 19-26)
POLAND 3, USA 0 (15-9, 15-7, 15-11) @ Wichita, KS.

USA 3, POLAND 1 (5-15, 15-3, 15-9, 15-11) @ Provo, UT.
POLAND 3, USA 2 (15-5, 10-15, 13-15, 15-13, 15-12) @ Stockton, CA.
USA 3, POLAND 1 (14-16, 15-10, 15-6, 15-6) @ Long Beach, CA.
USA 3, POLAND 0 (15-7, 15-12, 15-6) @ Santa Barbara, CA.
POLAND 3, USA 2 (15-10, 13-15, 5-15, 15-7, 15-5) @ San Diego, CA.

"We finish preparations for World Championships with a 3-3 split with Poland. They go on to a 6th in World's — we are ahead of the Poles!! Included in this tour is a very emotional victory at the Long Beach Arena."

1982 WORLD CHAMPIONSHIPS: ARGENTINA
(October 2-15)
BULGARIA 3, USA 2 (13-15, 15-6, 12-15, 15-11, 16-14)
USSR 3, USA 0 (15-11, 15-12, 16-14)
USA 3, CHILE 0 (15-1, 15-1, 15-5)
USA 3, LIBYA 0 (15-7, 15-1, 15-3)
USA 3, VENEZUELA 0 (15-2, 15-4, 15-8)
USA 3, IRAQ 0 (15-9, 15-6, 15-9)
USA 3, RUMANIA 1 (15-11, 13-15, 15-11, 15-10)
USA 3, FRANCE 0 (15-6, 15-4, 15-11)
USA 3, ITALY 0 (15-10, 15-5, 15-6)

"The single most disappointing loss of my life — to Bulgaria, up 12-5 in the 5th game. Platonov can't believe we lose the game, he asks me how, I shrug; I ask him how, he shrugs; we walk away. The next day we are close in a 3-game loss to the Soviets — our first effort at them in 3 years. We get closer every time we see them till May of '84. We cruise to a 13th finish, about 10 places too low."

USA VS. JAPAN MICHELOB LIGHT FRIENDSHIP TOUR:
(October 19-24)
USA 3, JAPAN 1 (15-12, 15-10, 13-15, 15-3) @ Glen Falls, NY.
USA 3, JAPAN 2 (16-14, 13-15, 11-15, 15-10, 15-12) @ Hackensack, NJ.
USA 3, JAPAN 2 (9-15, 15-3, 7-15, 15-13, 15-9) @ Keene, NH.
USA 3, JAPAN 0 (15-9, 15-10, 15-12) @ Worcester, MA.
USA 3, JAPAN 2 (15-11, 8-15, 15-12, 11-15, 15-12) @ Syracuse, NY.

"Japan is ours!! (Without Dvorak we go 5-0; they are off a 4th-place finish in World's!)."

1982 OVERALL RECORD: 45-15
RECORD IN U.S.: 22-6

1983 RESULTS

TOUR OF CUBA:
(April 4-10)
CUBA 3, USA 1 (15-7, 9-15, 15-4, 15-13) @ Santa Clara, CA.
CUBA 3, USA 2 (15-13, 12-15, 15-9, 11-15, 15-12) @ Santa Clara, CA.
CUBA 3, USA 0 (15-6, 15-11, 15-12) @ Santa Clara, CA.
USA 3, CUBA 0 (15-12, 15-8, 15-9) @ Santa Clara, CA.
CUBA 3, USA 0 (15-6, 15-6, 15-3) @ Havana

"Our first venture onto the volleyball court after Outward Bound! Lots of changes, the team struggles, Cuba is ahead of us here, we must learn and become comfortable with our new system!"

USA VS. CANADA:
(April 23-28)
USA 3, CANADA 2 (15-10, 5-15, 15-1, 14-16, 15-12) @ Knoxville, TN.

USA 3, CANADA 0 (15-10, 15-13, 15-8) @ Louisville, KY.
USA 3, CANADA 0 (15-8, 15-10, 15-6) @ Dayton, OH.
USA 3, CANADA 1 (16-14, 8-15, 15-12, 15-13) @ Lexington, KY.

"Canada still can't touch us!"

TOUR OF FINLAND:
(June 15-19)
USA 3, FINLAND 2 (15-5, 6-15, 15-10, 13-15, 16-14) @ Hameenleena
USA 3, FINLAND 0 (15-7, 15-12, 15-11) @ Helsinki
USA 3, FINLAND 1 (10-15, 15-13, 15-9, 15-4) @ Lapua
USA 3, FINLAND 2 (15-10, 8-15, 15-9, 14-16, 15-7) @ Seinajoki

TOUR OF POLAND:
(June 23-28)
USA 3, POLAND 2 (9-15, 15-9, 11-15, 15-9, 15-9) @ Katowicie
POLAND 3, USA 0 (15-7, 16-14, 15-11) @ Opole
USA 3, POLAND 0 (18-16, 15-11, 15-11) @ Wroclaw
USA 3, POLAND 1 (16-14, 15-2, 4-15, 15-9) @ Poznan
POLAND 3, USA 0 (15-13, 15-7, 15-10) @ Lodz

"We prepare for our zone championship by winning 4 in Finland (without Kiraly) and winning the series from the Poles on their home ground — our system is catching on!"

NORCECA ZONE CHAMPIONSHIPS: INDIANAPOLIS, INDIANA
(July 12-16)
USA 3, PUERTO RICO 0 (15-2, 15-2, 15-4)
USA 3, CANADA 0 (15-5, 15-6, 15-10)
USA 3, NETHERLAND ANTILLES 0 (15-2, 15-10, 15-6)
USA 3, MEXICO 0 (15-5, 15-6, 15-0)
USA 3, CUBA 0 (15-8, 15-5, 15-6)

"No one even challenged us — everything was smooth, a little too smooth."

USA VS BULGARIA MICHELOB LIGHT FRIENDSHIP TOUR:
(August 1-7)
USA 3, BULGARIA 1 (15-10, 15-8, 12-15, 15-12) @ Pocatello, ID.
USA 3, BULGARIA 0 (15-12, 15-10, 15-6) @ Great Falls, MT.
USA 3, BULGARIA 1 (15-12, 15-2, 13-15, 15-7) @ Santa Barbara, CA.
USA 3, BULGARIA 0 (15-8, 17-15, 15-10) @ San Diego, CA.

"Sweet Revenge!!"

QUEST FOR GOLD PRE-OLYMPIC TOURNAMENT: LONG BEACH ARENA
(August 9-13)
USA 3, JAPAN 1 (15-9, 15-17, 15-6, 15-5)
USA 3, ARGENTINA 0 (15-11, 15-10, 16-14)
USA 3, CANADA 2 (15-4, 7-15, 15-9, 12-15, 15-2)
JAPAN 3, USA 2 (15-10, 9-15, 15-12, 8-15, 15-3)

"Canada almost sneaks up on us, and Japan does for their last hurrah! The team needs a break from the emotional and physical strain!"

PAN AMERICAN GAMES: CARACAS, VENEZUELA
(August 18-27) — 2nd Team
CUBA 3, USA 0 (15-8, 15-7, 15-13)
USA 3, VENEZUELA 0 (15-11, 15-8, 15-4)

BRAZIL 3, USA 1 (15-11, 16-18, 15-10, 15-10)
USA 3, ARGENTINA 1 (13-15, 16-14, 15-12, 15-6)
USA 3, CANADA 1 (15-6, 8-15, 15-5, 15-12)
BRAZIL 3, USA 0 (15-10, 15-12, 15-12)
ARGENTINA 3, USA 0 (15-9, 15-9, 15-8)

SAVVINE INVITATIONAL TOURNAMENT: ODESSA, USSR
(August 23-30) — 1st Team
USA 3, CUBA 0 (15-11, 15-9, 15-6)
USA 3, FINLAND 0 (15-11, 15-6, 15-8)
USA 3, CZECHOSLOVAKIA 0 (15-6, 15-4, 15-6)
USSR 3, USA 1 (15-13, 14-16, 15-3, 15-11)
USA 3, POLAND 0 (15-9, 15-13, 15-5)
USA 3, JAPAN 2 (13-15, 15-7, 15-11, 8-15, 15-7)

"We are closing in on the USSR, and we're better than everyone else — it's been a long summer."

TOUR OF JAPAN:
(September 17-24)
JAPAN 3, USA 2 (15-13, 15-4, 11-15, 8-15, 15-6) @ Koofu
JAPAN 3, USA 1 (15-11, 7-15, 15-11, 15-7) @ Mito
USA 3, JAPAN 0 (15-10, 15-5, 15-11) @ Kooriyama
USA 3, JAPAN 0 (15-4, 15-13, 15-10) @ Chino
USA 3, JAPAN 2 (7-15, 9-15, 15-4, 15-10, 15-4) @ Nagoya
JAPAN 3, USA 2 (15-12, 15-9, 15-17, 7-15, 16-14) @ Osaka

"No motivation to play, but Japan is still very tough at home."

USA VS POLAND MICHELOB LIGHT FRIENDSHIP TOUR:
(October 13-21)
USA 3, POLAND 0 (15-8, 15-6, 15-4) @ San Diego, CA.
USA 3, POLAND 2 (14-16, 15-7, 15-13, 5-15, 15-7) @ Des Moines, IA.
USA 3, POLAND 2 (15-8, 9-15, 15-13, 13-15, 15-13) @ Hartford, CT.
USA 3, POLAND 2 (9-15, 15-11, 14-16, 15-12, 15-8) @ Elizabethtown, PA.
USA 3, POLAND 0 (15-7, 15-13, 15-7) @ Elizabeth, NJ.

CANADA CUP TOURNAMENT: SHERBROOKE, QUEBEC
(October 23-29)
CUBA 3, USA 0 (15-9, 16-14, 15-11)
USA 3, CANADA 1 (15-10, 7-15, 16-14, 15-9)
USA 3, POLAND 0 (15-13, 15-2, 15-11)
USA 3, POLAND 0 (15-9, 15-11, 15-13)
USA 3, CUBA 0 (16-14, 15-7, 15-1)

"We end '83 like '81 with a great win over Cuba in the Canada Cup Tournament! The team is beginning to perform under pressure."

1983 OVERALL RECORD: 44-16
RECORD IN U.S.: 21-1

1984 RESULTS

TOUR OF CUBA:
(February 6-14)
CUBA 3, USA 1 (15-11, 15-7, 13-15, 15-10) @ Havana

USA 3, CUBA 2 (11-15, 16-14, 15-7, 8-15, 15-10) @ Havana
CUBA 3, USA 1 (15-11, 15-4, 13-15, 15-2) @ Havana
CUBA 3, USA 2 (11-15, 15-9, 12-15, 18-16, 15-10) @ Havana
USA 3, CUBA 0 (15-13, 15-12, 16-14) @ Havana
CUBA 3, USA 1 (15-8, 10-15, 16-14, 15-7) @ Havana

"We start the Olympic year in Cuba, with same tough matches, some injuries and the emergence of Timmons — the last fact is most significant!"

USA VS. CUBA
(March 2-9)
USA 3, CUBA 0 (16-14, 16-14, 16-14) @ Santa Barbara, CA.
CUBA 3, USA 1 (7-15, 15-13, 15-6, 15-8) @ Butte, MT.
CUBA 3, USA 2 (13-15, 9-15, 15-9, 15-9, 15-11) @ Bozeman, MT.
CUBA 3, USA 1 (15-11, 5-15, 15-13, 19-17) @ Billings, MT.
USA 3, CUBA 2 (15-10, 8-15, 15-10, 11-15, 15-10) @ Great Falls, MT.
USA 3, CUBA 2 (12-15, 15-6, 5-15, 15-9, 15-8) @ San Diego, CA.

"Cuba comes to the United States. We split. We are adjusting to our continuing injuries, and Timmons is still great!"

USA VS. CZECHOSLOVAKIA MICHELOB LIGHT FRIENDSHIP TOUR:
(March 24-27)
USA 3, CSSR 0 (15-2, 15-12, 15-7) @ San Diego, CA.
USA 3, CSSR 1 (15-12, 17-15, 9-15, 15-6) @ Tucson, AZ.
USA 3, CSSR 1 (15-11, 9-15, 15-9, 16-14) @ Phoenix, AZ.

CHAMPIONSHIP SERIES TOURNAMENT:
(March 30-April 7)
USA 3, JAPAN 0 (15-1, 15-5, 15-7) @ Las Vegas, NV.
CANADA 3, USA 2 (11-15, 13-15, 15-10, 15-13, 15-13) @ Las Vegas, NV.
CANADA 3, USA 1 (12-15, 15-4, 15-7, 15-3) @ Santa Barbara, CA.
USA 3, JAPAN 0 (15-3, 15-11, 15-11) @ Santa Barbara, CA.
USA 3, CSSR 1 (13-15, 15-4, 15-7, 15-13) @ Long Beach, CA.
USA 3, CANADA 0 (15-13, 15-5, 15-7) @ Long Beach, CA.
USA 3, JAPAN 0 (15-4, 15-12, 15-12) @ Honolulu, HI.

"Canada wins this competition; they finally catch our number. We are without 5 starters! It will be our last loss for 28 matches over 4 months."

TOUR OF BULGARIA:
(May 4-5)
USA 3, BULGARIA 2 (6-15, 15-5, 15-10, 12-15, 16-14) @ Sofia
USA 3, BULGARIA 1 (15-9, 15-13, 15-17, 15-7) @ Sofia

TOUR OF USSR:
(May 8-13)
USA 3, USSR 2 (11-15, 15-5, 13-15, 16-14, 15-6) ** @ Kharkov
USA 3, USSR 0 (15-10, 15-11, 15-10) @ Kharkov
USA 3, USSR 0 (15-7, 15-9, 15-12) @ Kharkov
USA 3, USSR 0 (15-11, 15-2, 15-10) @ Kharkov

** "We are on top; first win since 1968, the BOYCOTT!! Wilde breaks his leg. Too many highs and lows."

TOURNAMENT IN CZECHOSLOVAKIA: BANSKA BYSTRICIA
(May 16-20)
USA 3, USSR 'B' 1 (10-15, 15-7, 15-13, 15-13)
USA 3, CSSR 1 (15-11, 13-15, 15-9, 15-8)
USA 3, CSSR 'B' 0 (15-11, 15-8, 15-10)
USA 3, FINLAND 0 (15-13, 15-9, 15-5)
USA 3, BULGARIA 1 (6-15, 15-8, 15-9, 15-9)

"We're rolling now!"

TOUR OF JAPAN:
(May 30-June 3)
USA 3, JAPAN 2 (12-15, 15-12, 14-16, 15-4, 15-4) @ Tokyo
USA 3, JAPAN 2 (10-15, 17-15, 14-16, 15-12, 15-8) @ Toyama
USA 3, JAPAN 0 (15-11, 15-10, 15-13) @ Nagaya

"We sweep in Japan!!"

USA VS. CHINA:
(June 15-18)
USA 3, CHINA 0 (15-0, 15-1, 17-15) @ Boca Raton, FL.
USA 3, CHINA 0 (15-10, 15-7, 15-12) @ New York, NY.
USA 3, CHINA 1 (15-5, 15-7, 11-15, 15-8) @ St. Louis, MO.

USA CUP TOURNAMENT: SAN DIEGO, CA.
(June 22-24)
USA 3, ARGENTINA 0 (15-8, 15-5, 15-6)
USA 3, CHINA 0 (15-8, 15-11, 15-5)
USA 3, COLLEGE STARS 0 (15-2, 15-1, 15-11)

USA VS. ARGENTINA:
(June 27)
USA 3, ARGENTINA 0 (15-7, 15-7, 17-15) @ San Francisco, CA.

"Last match before Pullman and final training — the team is hot, bring on the Olympics!!"

1984 OVERALL RECORD: 39-10 (Including Olympics)
RECORD IN U.S.: 23-6

1984 OLYMPIC RESULTS

ROUND ROBIN

July 29

KOREA 3, TUNISIA 0 (15-7, 15-7, 15-7)
JAPAN 3, CHINA 0 (15-9, 15-9, 15-8)
USA 3, ARGENTINA 1 (15-6, 15-7, 10-15, 15-8)
ITALY 3, CANADA 1 (10-15, 15-4, 15-6, 15-7)

July 31

CANADA 3, EGYPT 0 (15-10, 15-9, 15-3)
ITALY 3, CHINA 0 (15-5, 16-14, 15-13)
BRAZIL 3, ARGENTINA 1 (15-8, 15-8, 15-17, 16-14)
USA 3, TUNISIA 0 (15-3, 15-2, 15-3)

August 2

CHINA 3, EGYPT 0 (15-3, 15-5, 18-16)
BRAZIL 3, TUNISIA 0 (15-5, 15-9, 15-2)
JAPAN 3, ITALY 2 (5-15, 11-15, 15-10, 15-10, 16-14)
USA 3, KOREA 0 (15-13, 15-9, 15-6)

August 4

ARGENTINA 3, TUNISIA 0 (15-9, 15-7, 15-3)
KOREA 3, BRAZIL 1 (15-4, 15-13, 13-15, 15-8)
JAPAN 3, EGYPT 0 (15-6, 15-10, 15-11)
CANADA 3, CHINA 0 (15-8, 15-7, 15-3)

August 6

KOREA 3, ARGENTINA 2 (15-6, 14-16, 13-15, 15-7, 15-12)
CANADA 3, JAPAN 0 (15-10, 15-8, 15-9)
ITALY 3, EGYPT 0 (15-4, 15-7, 15-6)
BRAZIL 3, USA 0 (15-10, 15-11, 15-2)

SEMI-FINALS

Places	August 8
5-8	KOREA 3, CHINA 1 (15-4, 15-11, 6-15, 19-17)
	ARGENTINA 3, JAPAN 1 (9-15, 15-10, 15-10, 15-11)
1-4	BRAZIL 3, ITALY 1 (12-15, 15-2, 15-3, 15-5)
	USA 3, CANADA 0 (15-6, 15-10, 15-7)

FINALS

Places	August 8
9-10	TUNISIA 3, EGYPT 2 (15-13, 15-9, 5-15, 13-15, 15-5)

August 10

| 7-8 | JAPAN 3, CHINA 0 (16-4, 15-9, 15-6) |
| 5-6 | KOREA 3, ARGENTINA 1 (15-13, 8-15, 15-9, 15-7) |

August 11 (Medal Matches)

| 3-4 | ITALY 3, CANADA 0 (15-11, 15-12, 15-8) |
| 1-2 | USA 3, BRAZIL 0 (15-6, 15-6, 15-7) |

OLYMPIC GAMES: FINAL RESULTS

	Matches	Games	Points
GOLD — USA	5-1	15-4	258-159
SILVER — BRAZIL	4-2	13-8	267-214
BRONZE — ITALY	4-2	15-7	280-234
4TH — CANADA	3-3	10-9	221-212
5TH — KOREA	5-1	15-8	312-253
6TH — ARGENTINA	2-4	11-13	282-307

7TH — JAPAN	4-2	13-8	271-245
8TH — CHINA	1-5	4-15	203-261
9TH — TUNISIA	1-4	3-14	127-237
10TH — EGYPT	0-5	2-15	147-246

POST OLYMPIC COMPETITION – 1984 RESULTS

SEOUL INVITATIONAL TOURNAMENT: SEOUL, KOREA
(October 25-November 1)
USA 3, JAPAN 1 (15-3, 15-4, 16-18, 15-5)
USA 3, MEXICO 0 (15-2, 15-6, 15-11)
USA 3, KOREA 1 (12-15, 15-8, 15-11, 15-11)
USA 3, MEXICO 0 (15-8, 15-10, 15-4)
USA 3, KOREA 1 (2-15, 15-12, 15-12, 15-13)

"The USA is still very good without Dvorak, Salmons, Waldie, Sunderland, Duwelius, and Marlowe! Timmons tears up his knee in a win over Korea for tournament Gold!"

JAPAN CUP WORLD TOURNAMENT:
(November 7-15)
USA 3, KOREA 0 (15-10, 15-9, 15-6) @ Tokyo
USA 3, POLAND 1 (15-6, 13-15, 15-2, 15-11) @ Tokyo
USSR 3, USA 2 (12-15, 13-15, 15-8, 15-8, 15-11) @ Kyoto
USA 3, JAPAN 0 (15-9, 15-3, 15-11) @ Osaka
USA 3, CHINA 1 (15-5, 15-5, 12-15, 15-2) @ Kobe
USA 3, BULGARIA 0 (15-9, 15-10, 15-10) @ Hiroshima
USA 3, MEXICO 0 (15-7, 15-6, 15-10) @ Hiroshima

"The USA goes to this tournament and answers the critics of the boycotting countries. We crush Poland and Bulgaria, lose a tight match to the USSR, and, along with the Soviets dominate the field. (We are, of course, without half of our Olympic team)."

TOUR OF BRAZIL:
(November 20-25)
BRAZIL 3, USA 0 (15-16, 15-10, 15-9) @ Sao Paolo
BRAZIL 3, USA 0 (16-14, 15-12, 16-14) @ Belo Horizonte
BRAZIL 3, USA 2 (10-15, 13-15, 15-11, 17-15, 15-7) @ Porto Alegre
USA 3, BRAZIL 0 (15-11, 16-14, 15-7) @ Brazilia

"Brazil wants revenge and gets it! They have their entire Silver Medal team. They beat us outdoors in the mist before 47,000 fans! We finally solve their home court edge before 25,000 in Brazilia."

USA VS BRAZIL:
(November 28-December 9)
USA 3, BRAZIL 0 (16-14, 15-7, 15-12) @ Princeton, NJ
BRAZIL 3, USA 0 (15-8, 15-11, 15-12) @ Providence, RI.
USA 3, BRAZIL 0 (15-6, 18-16, 15-11) @ Boston, MA.
USA 3, BRAZIL 1 (15-8, 15-13, 12-15, 16-14) @ Chicago, IL.
BRAZIL 3, USA 0 (15-11, 15-12, 15-11) @ Indianapolis, IN.
USA 3, BRAZIL 1 (19-17, 15-10, 7-15, 15-3) @ Dayton, OH.
BRAZIL 3, USA 2 (6-15, 17-15, 15-11, 6-15, 16-14) @ Las Vegas, NV.
BRAZIL 3, USA 1 (32-35, 35-32, 42-40, 35-28)* @ Long Beach, CA.
USA 3, BRAZIL 2 (13-15, 15-9, 15-9, 10-15, 15-5) @ San Francisco, CA.

* New experimental scoring system tried.

"We bring Brazil to the USA for a coast-to-coast promotional tour. We eke out a 5-4 match win (remember our first tour in '81) and play before almost 55,000 new volleyball fans."

1984 OVERALL RECORD: 56-18
RECORD IN U.S.: 28-10

OLYMPIC MEDALISTS — MEN

TOKYO — 1964

1 USSR
2 CZECHOSLOVAKIA
3 JAPAN

MEXICO CITY — 1968

1 USSR
2 JAPAN
3 CZECHOSLOVAKIA

MUNICH — 1972

1 JAPAN
2 EAST GERMANY
3 USSR

MONTREAL — 1976

1 POLAND
2 USSR
3 CUBA

MOSCOW — 1980

1 USSR
2 BULGARIA
3 RUMANIA

LOS ANGELES — 1984

1 USA
2 BRAZIL
3 ITALY

1984 USA
Men's Olympic Team

Name	No.	HT(CM)	WT(KG)	Date of Birth
Berzins, Aldis	12	6-2(189)	172(78)	10-3-56
Blanchard, Mike (Alternate)	11	6-5(198)	194(88)	12-5-56
Buck, Craig	7	6-8(203)	210(96)	8-24-58
Duwelius, Rich	5	6-6(198)	195(89)	11-23-54
Dvorak, Dusty	1	6-3(190)	180(82)	7-29-58
Kiraly, Karch	15	6-3(191)	190(86)	11-3-60
Marlowe, Chris — Captain	10	6-3(194)	190(86)	9-28-51
Powers, Pat	13	6-5(197)	200(91)	2-13-58
Salmons, Steve	3	6-4(195)	205(93)	7-3-58
Saunders, Dave	2	6-3(191)	180(82)	10-19-60
Sunderland, Paul	4	6-4(198)	190(86)	3-29-52
Timmons, Steve	6	6-5(199)	205(93)	11-29-58
Waldie, Marc	9	6-4(195)	185(84)	8-24-55
Wilde, Rod (Alternate)	8	6-1(187)	165(75)	11-4-56

Head Coach — Doug Beal
Assistant Coach — Bill Neville
Assistant Coach — Tony Crabb